TWENTIETH CENTURY THEMES

General Editor: JAMES L. HENDERSON

Poverty and Affluence

*An Introduction to the International Relations
of Rich and Poor Economies*

BY

SARAH CHILD

HAMISH HAMILTON
LONDON

First published in Great Britain, 1968
by Hamish Hamilton Ltd.
90 Great Russell Street, London, W.C.1
© *1968 by Sarah Child*

SBN   241   91449   3

(

Printed in Great Britain by
Western Printing Services Ltd, Bristol

POVERTY AND AFFLUENCE

Contents

Preface   9

WORLD ECONOMIC STRUCTURE

1. THE THREE GROUPS OF ECONOMIES   13
2. RESOURCES, PRODUCTION AND CONSUMPTION   20
3. INTERNATIONAL TRADE AND CAPITAL   29
   MOVEMENTS

THE EMERGENCE OF THE PRESENT STRUCTURE

4. THE NINETEENTH-CENTURY INDUSTRIAL
   REVOLUTION   45
5. THE ROLE OF GOVERNMENTS IN WESTERN
   INDUSTRIALIZATION   52
6. THE COMMUNIST ECONOMIES AND
   INDUSTRIALIZATION   61
7. THE DEVELOPED ECONOMIES BETWEEN THE
   WARS   76
8. THE UNDERDEVELOPED COUNTRIES' COLONIAL
   BACKGROUND   86
9. THE THREE GROUPS OF ECONOMIES SINCE 1945   101

WORLD ECONOMIC PROBLEMS— PROGRESS TOWARDS SOLUTIONS

10. THE OUTSTANDING PROBLEMS   121
11. AID TO UNDERDEVELOPED COUNTRIES   130
12. THE LIBERALIZATION OF WORLD TRADE   145
13. INTERNATIONAL COMMODITY AGREEMENTS   161
14. INTERNATIONAL MONETARY REFORM   174
15. THE PROBLEMS OF THE RICH   191

Bibliography and Further Reading   203

Index   205

5

List of Tables

1. Gross National Incomes   16
2. Two Patterns of Consumption   28
3. A Breakdown of World Exports   34
4. US Private Direct Investment Abroad   38
5. Aid Disbursed from OECD   133
6. Official Bilateral Commitments   134
7. Principal Donors and Recipients of Net Bilateral Aid   136
8. World Reserves and IMF Positions   179

Acknowledgments

This book owes a great deal to the suggestions and criticisms of my husband, R. N. Wood, B.A., at present Senior Economist in the Ministry of Economic Affairs and Development Planning, Tanzania, who also contributed Chapter 11 'Aid to Underdeveloped Countries'.

Chapter 13 'International Commodity Agreements' was written by Nicholas Monck, B.A., who is at present on secondment from H.M. Treasury as Senior Economist, Ministry of Agriculture, Tanzania.

Preface

The world which we inhabit makes sense.

This is the conviction on which the volumes in this series are based. Despite two world wars, several regional wars now in progress, the threat of nuclear annihilation and the menacing food and population problems, there is evidence that, in the words of an Indian statesman and philosopher, 'The world which has found itself as a single body is feeling for its soul.'

Why should the rich nations help the poor?

Poverty and Affluence in answering this question, examines against a background of recent economic development, the relationship between the rich nations who represent roughly one-sixth of the world's population, and the poor nations. The book discusses the major economic and social problems of both societies such as increasing public squalor in the rich countries, and the lack of skilled manpower and the rapid growth of population which stifle the progress of the poor countries. Moreover, there is a full account of the suggested reforms of the world monetary system, and of the recent gold crisis.

PART ONE

WORLD ECONOMIC STRUCTURE

CHAPTER ONE

The Three Groups of Economies

An economy is a unit which produces goods and services on the one hand and consumes them on the other. The term can apply to a village, a town, a country or to the world as a whole, but it is most often used of countries. In practice the geographical boundaries of states often make little economic sense. The people living on either side of a frontier are frequently engaged in identical economic activities, and there are seldom economic reasons for a boundary to be where it is; in other cases production on one side may be totally dependent on some process on the other side if it is to have any utility. Such examples are most common among the ex-colonial territories of Africa which the European powers divided up among themselves. Roland Oliver and J. D. Fage described this late nineteenth-century process well in their *Short History of Africa*[1]—'Statesmen and diplomats met in offices and country houses and drew lines across maps which themselves were usually inaccurate. Often the lack of geographical detail was such that frontiers had to be traced along lines of latitude and longitude.' In older states more natural boundaries have tended to evolve. As a result of the activities of modern governments it is convenient to equate a political organization with an economy, and to consider how it is that the inhabitants of a particular country get their living, through the production of goods and services for their own use and by selling them abroad in exchange for imports.

Economies, like the political structures behind them, vary enormously in size, complexity and organization. In the mid-twentieth-century world, political and economic factors coincide

[1] Penguin African Library, 1962.

in allocating them to three main groups—the developed, the underdeveloped and the communist or centrally planned. The definitions of these groups are vague and overlapping, and the communist countries can themselves be divided between the developed and the underdeveloped. Broadly speaking, the developed countries are rich; that is to say that the national income of any one of them, when divided by the population, works out at several hundred US dollars per head, although in very few countries is the national income distributed in such a way as to eliminate poverty altogether. They are in general industrialized countries, with the greater part of their national output derived from manufacturing, and with only a minority of the labour force engaged in agriculture (although there are exceptions to this, such as New Zealand). They have large stocks of capital, which consist not only of such assets as roads, railways, power stations, factories and machinery, but also of educated and skilled people.

The underdeveloped countries are poor, though with varying degrees of poverty. Their national incomes tend to be even less well distributed than those of the developed countries, so that their poorest inhabitants are very poor indeed. They are usually still primary economies, i.e. engaged in producing agricultural and other 'natural' commodities, and the majority of the labour force is usually employed on the land. They have little capital in the form of such things as roads and railways, and are severely short of educated people. With their low income levels, almost all earnings are needed simply to keep the population alive, and there is little to spare for the savings necessary to break out of this situation. A rapid rate of population growth normally completes the vicious circle.

The communist economies are distinguished from the rest mainly by the government's role in planning and owning production and trade. The extent of government ownership varies, but it is always very large. The extent and effectiveness of planning also varies, but it is far more detailed and authoritarian than anywhere else. The aim of communist planning is the rapid development of the economy, and to this end a very large part of national output is earmarked for productive investment. As a corollary, the satisfaction of consumers' wants is given a low priority. Today's generation is required to forgo such satisfaction for the sake of those to come. Investment for the sake of investment is not of course a sufficient condition for economic growth; some types of investment are more productive than others, and it is not always easy to tell in advance which are likely to yield the highest benefits. While some of these economies have achieved high rates of growth, in others, such as Czechoslovakia until very recently, production has stagnated.

The communist economies identify themselves. It is much less easy to allocate countries between the first two groups of economies, or to say precisely on what grounds this should be done. No particular level of economic expansion can be fixed at which an economy becomes a developed one. Western Europe is always considered to be a developed region, but if income per head is taken as the main criterion of development, there are countries in Europe, such as Portugal and Greece, which are as poor or poorer than some of the countries of Latin America, which are usually classified as underdeveloped; the point at which the income line is drawn must in any case always be arbitrary. Countries whose classification as developed is unquestioned—the USA, Canada, the rich countries of Northern Europe and Australia and New Zealand—all have incomes per head of well over US $1,000 (£357) a year. Countries which are undoubtedly underdeveloped, like India or Kenya, have incomes per head of well under US $100 (£36). But many countries fall within this vast gap—Italy, for example, which has less than US $1,000 a year per head and includes a large underdeveloped region, but which is not considered to be an underdeveloped country; Venezuela, which has a larger income per head than Italy, but which usually is; Japan, with less than half the income per head of the UK and appreciably less than Venezuela, but with a degree of industrialization which ranks it as a developed country. Moreover there are considerable difficulties involved in collecting comparable information about the income levels of different countries. National income is the sum of all the earnings made over the year in an economy— the wages earned by employees, the profits made by enterprises, the interest earned on capital and the rent on property. There are many problems about its assessment in a developed economy, where it can be largely measured in terms of monetary transactions, but these problems are far greater in an underdeveloped economy in which a large part of production is that of peasant farmers, who eat most of what they produce themselves. However, the table below shows some examples of the calculations which have been made.

TABLE 1

Gross National Income per head in certain regions
and countries, 1964 US $)

US	3002	Latin American average*	345
Canada	1987	Venezuela*	881
West European average	1150	Bolivia*	125
Sweden	2013	Ghana	232
UK	1472	Kenya	85
Italy	847	Malawi*	43
Portugal	333	East and S.E. Asian average†*	92
Australia	1688	India	82
New Zealand	1749	Japan	590

* 1963.   † Excluding Japan.

Source: *UN Yearbook of National Accounts Statistics.*

It is not possible to make comparable estimates of national income per head in the communist countries, where national income is computed in different ways and many prices (particularly foreign exchange rates) are arbitrarily fixed by the government. The latest official Soviet estimate of income per head in the USSR in comparison with the USA was made in 1963, when it was calculated to be just over 50 per cent of the American level. Most independent Western estimates assess the difference as even greater, for one reason because the Soviet calculation of national income is limited to the value of the output of goods and excludes services. The value of the output of the service industries is proportionately greater in a rich country, where consumers can afford to spend a substantial proportion of their incomes on entertainments, holidays and restaurants, and the varied range of consumer goods calls for many more shops and people to sell them. If comparable information were available, it seems probable that the national incomes of the USSR, East Germany and Czechoslovakia would work out at 'developed' country levels, or at over $1,000 per head, although, since a smaller proportion of national income is distributed to consumers in these countries than is usual in western economies, average standards of living would in fact be lower than in western countries at similar levels. The other communist countries would fall among the richer of the underdeveloped countries, except for Bulgaria and Albania, which are much poorer than the rest, while China is among the poorest.

The countries which fall clearly into the category of the developed are the US and Canada, most of Western Europe, Australia and New Zealand. On the grounds of their degree of industrialization, Japan and South Africa are usually also included. More doubtful cases are Greece, Portugal, Yugoslavia and Israel, which might all be described as 'developing', except that this adjective is now frequently used as a substitute for 'underdeveloped', as being more encouraging for the countries concerned. The USSR is by most definitions, and particularly in view of its stock of capital, a developed country, as are East Germany and Czechoslovakia; the other East European countries are more marginal cases. The underdeveloped countries constitute the rest of the world, with the poorest to be found in Asia and Africa, and the relatively better off in Latin America.

According to the theory of Professor W. W. Rostow, economies evolve through five stages. These he identifies as 'the traditional society', 'the pre-conditions for take-off', 'the take-off', 'the drive to maturity', and 'the age of mass-consumption'. The period of take-off is a time of high saving and investment, at a rate of not less than a tenth of national income, which enables the economy concerned to build up its capital stock of roads, railways, water and power supplies and educational facilities (the economic infrastructure, to give this its technical term) and then to make productive investment in factories and machinery. After this economic growth becomes a self-sustaining process, whereas countries in the first two stages can only experience sporadic ups and downs, the result of good or bad harvests and similar uncontrollable factors. In practice, economies tend to show awkward individual characteristics which make it hard to fit them exactly into any one of these stages. Nevertheless it is sometimes useful to think of economic progress in terms of this historical development. In some underdeveloped countries it is easy to recognize Professor Rostow's description of the pre-conditions for take-off, where the traditional agricultural society has begun to change under the impact of new ideas. 'New types of enter-prising men come forward . . . willing to mobilize savings and to take risks in pursuit of profit or modernization. Banks and other institutions for mobilizing capital appear. Investment increases, notably in transport, communications and in raw materials in which other nations may have an economic interest . . . here and there, modern manufacturing enterprise appears, using the new methods. But all this activity proceeds at a limited pace within an economy and a society characterized by traditional low-produc-tivity methods, by the old social structure and values.'[1] In many others, the old social structure has already been shattered, some-times with the accompaniment of the characteristics of an econo-mic 'take-off', and sometimes not. But for all underdeveloped countries the goal of economic maturity has now become distinct, and rapid progress away from the traditional society a political necessity.

During the first half of this century, most governments in Europe and North America were under pressure to reduce the contrasts between the standards of living of the rich and the poor in their own countries. In the second half of the century, for the first time in world history, pressure is being exerted to reduce such differences between countries as well as within them. The motives for this international concern are mixed. On the one hand there is concern with injustice and suffering, and the modern revolution in communications has led to almost as great an awareness of such conditions abroad as of those at home. On the other hand, just as poverty in Europe earlier in the century was seen as a potential cause of revolution, poverty abroad is now considered a threat to world political stability. The end of the

[1] W. W. Rostow, *The Stages of Economic Growth*, Cambridge University Press, 1950.

colonial system has opened the poorer countries of the world to the influence of the world as a whole, and the existence of two rival world political systems ensures the interest of the leaders of both in the countries which are so far uncommitted.

CHAPTER TWO

Resources, Production and Consumption

ECONOMIC RESOURCES

The explanation of why a particular country is rich or poor is only partly a matter of economic analysis. The country's history, its political and social structure, and often the history and politics of neighbouring countries as well, all constitute the background to the economic scene. Nevertheless, in attempting to account for national wealth or national poverty, the economic resources available to the country concerned are a good starting point. The history of the use which it has made of such resources is a country's economic history.

The basic economic resources are land, labour and capital. An economy's labour force is that part of the population which is of working age. Its usefulness varies with the extent to which it is employed, with current levels of education and experience in various skills, and sometimes with natural abilities; the Chinese and Japanese, for instance, appear to be more manually dexterous than other races, so that they can learn skilled manual work (such as assembling a transistor radio) more quickly and make fewer mistakes than others. 'Land' in economics is used in the broad sense of all natural resources—land suitable for agriculture, mineral deposits, forests, fishing waters or water power. The value of an economy's resources of labour and land depends heavily on their relationship to each other or on the availability of the third factor, capital. A large labour force is an asset in relation to a large supply of agricultural land or a large stock of factories and machinery for it to operate. In the absence of either of these it becomes a population problem. A mineral deposit is of no use unless there is labour to work it and in most cases the capital necessary to provide machinery and transport to where its output

20

can be used. Labour and land are both extremely unevenly distributed between the world's economies, but the poorer countries
are not usually poor in the quantity of labour available, nor are
they always short of natural resources.

The underdeveloped countries include about one-half of the
world's population of 3·3 billion (1965). Just over one-sixth lives
in the developed countries of Europe, North America, Japan,
Australia and New Zealand, while the communist countries of the
USSR, Eastern Europe and China account for the remaining
third. If the population were evenly distributed over the world's
land surface, there would be one square mile for every 62 people.
In fact the population is highly concentrated in some regions and
scattered in others. In the overcrowded continent of Europe,
13 per cent of the world's population occupies less than 4 per cent
of its land area, and the average number of people per square
mile is 231; in Western Europe it rises to 370. More than half the
world's population lives in Asia, which covers about a fifth of the
surface; mainland China has about 186 people to the square mile,
but India has 401 and Japan 679. At the other extreme, in Africa
less than 10 per cent of the world's population occupies over 20
per cent of its surface, and the average ranges from 41 in West
Africa to 13 in Central Africa; in Australia and New Zealand the
average falls to 5. North America and the USSR, which have very
similar populations and occupy almost the same land area (about
16 per cent of the world's surface in both cases), are also relatively
empty, each with about 16 people per square mile. The average is
higher in South America, with a similar land area, much of which
is still inaccessible jungle, and a rather larger population; certain
countries in South America, particularly in the Caribbean, are
among the overcrowded.

The distribution of natural resources between economies is
certainly even more erratic than the relationship between population and land area, but there are many difficulties involved in
measuring the natural resources available. In the case of agricultural land, for example, less than 10 per cent of the earth's land
surface is at present cultivated, but it has been estimated that at
least as much again could practicably be brought into cultivation
at costs which would vary widely, depending on the amount of

clearing, irrigation and fertilization necessary. Much of this potential lies in Africa and South America, in neither of which in many areas is land in short supply; in Asia, which is desperately short of agricultural land in relation to population, there is less extra potential, although areas of existing cultivation could be used much more intensively by means of expenditure on irrigation and fertilization. Knowledge of the world's mineral resources is still incomplete; estimates of the size and location of oil deposits in particular change appreciably every few years. However, as far as is known, very few countries are well equipped with all the natural resources basic to modern industrial development. Of the four traditionally the most important—coal, iron, water power and oil—only the USA and the USSR are known to have all four in quantity. Several European countries have iron and several have coal, but they are not often found together. China is now thought to have bigger reserves of coal than the USSR and possibly almost as much as the USA; Europe's coal reserves are much smaller, although European production is currently larger than that of the USA. Asia, apart from China, is believed to have little coal, although India and Japan have small amounts, and as far as is known the South African deposits are the only substantial reserve in Africa. The biggest reserves of iron ore are found in Brazil, India and Canada, and in Africa, which also makes up for its lack of coal with a big potential in water power. Over half the world's known reserves of petroleum are in the Middle East; the second largest share is in the USA, followed by the USSR and Canada. However, oil is more widely distributed than most important natural resources, for several European and South American countries, together with India, Burma, North Borneo, Trinidad, China, Nigeria, Libya and Egypt, are known to have at least small amounts.

Other key minerals are even more highly concentrated in a few areas. Over half the world's tin comes from Bolivia, Malaya and Indonesia; four-fifths of deposits of copper are in the USA, Chile, Zambia and the Congo. Two-thirds of all asbestos and over half of all nickel ore come from Canada; two-thirds of all cobalt from the Congo. Uranium, at present the main source of nuclear fuel, is found in quantity in North America, Europe, Africa and

Australia, but not in South America and only to a small extent in Asia. No developed country with a full range of modern industries is free from the necessity of importing some of these basic raw materials, although the USSR is more self-sufficient than most, and the USA more so than Europe or Japan.

PRODUCTION

For any one economy, it is not the actual level of supply of the various natural resources that determines the pattern of production, but their importance in relation to each other. To the extent that, within an economy, labour is free to move from one occupation to another, it will tend to go to the most profitable work. Thus a mineral deposit which is of such low quality that it would not be considered worth exploiting in one country may be mined in another, where the value of the output of the men employed in mining it is greater than the value of their work would be if they changed to any other occupation. India has less agricultural land per head, and of poorer quality, than the USA, but since agricultural land is in greater supply in India than any other resource, the majority of Indians are employed in agriculture and only a small minority of Americans. If there were no political and other obstacles to the movement of labour across frontiers, the world's natural resources would in theory eventually all be exploited down to a minimum uniform level of productivity. As it is, countries make the largest incomes they can by producing as much as possible of those commodities which are most valuable in relation to any others which can be produced at home.

It would, however, be a mistake to think that it is the presence or absence of valuable natural resources which distinguishes the rich from the poor countries. Japan is an example of a country short of almost everything except labour, yet it is one of the very few underdeveloped countries which in recent years has managed to join the ranks of the developed. The quantity and quality of the other two basic factors of production, capital and labour, are much more important. Most underdeveloped countries have plentiful supplies of labour, but not of the skilled and educated labour which is necessary for modern manufacturing, nor of the experienced managers needed to organize it. Developed countries, besides having a large supply of skilled labour and management (although in most developed economies at present the demand for skilled labour tends to run well ahead of supply), also have a high level of capital invested for every member of the labour force, in the form of a complex economic infrastructure, in factories and machinery, and in expenditure on scientific and technical research and the development of its results. The determination of which goods a developed economy can most profitably produce rests on a very complicated combination of the skills and enterprise available, the current level of technical innovation and the ability to make use of it by new investment. All production decisions are related principally to the factors of labour and capital; the availability of natural resources is no longer of much importance, since well-developed transport systems mean that almost any raw material can be brought to almost any factory site.

For the underdeveloped economies, natural resources are still the crucial factor in determining what is to be produced. The forms of primary production vary enormously—between agriculture and mining, between products which require little skill in growing or extracting and others which do, and between production by peasant small-holders and by large estates or other concerns. The importance of labour and capital is consequently also variable. Capital is, for example, essential in developing a copper industry, because the copper content of the ore is so small (the average in Zambia is about 3 per cent) that smelting needs to be carried out at the mine to avoid huge transport costs. To grow most of the crops of tropical and semi-tropical climates, on the other hand, very little capital is needed, since only small planting costs are involved. Growing and preparing tea requires intensive labour and a measure of skill; picking coconuts and drying them for copra is relatively simple. But whatever the skills and capital available, the nature of the local industries depends primarily on resources and climate, and since skills and capital are normally in short supply, where manufacturing industries exist, they are mainly those which do not require much skilled labour nor heavy capital investment.

Manufacturing which does require large quantities of capital and a high level of technical skill is largely concentrated in the developed countries. Well over 80 per cent of the world ouput of steel, the basic material of nearly all modern industrial processes, is for example produced in the USA, the UK and European Common Market countries, the USSR and Japan. China and India have both put considerable effort into developing their steel industries in recent years, but their production is still small. This concentration of production in a few developed countries is even more intensive for many capital goods (machinery and equipment for production) manufactured for industry, and for the more expensive 'durable consumer goods'—cars, washing machines, refrigerators and television sets. For most of these modern manufactures, production cannot be efficiently carried out on a small scale. In the motor industry, for example, the cost per car produced falls sharply up to the production of about 100,000 a year of the same model. The reasons for these 'returns to scale' lie sometimes in the complexity of the manufacturing process; if some hundreds of different operations are involved, for each of which a different group of workers must be trained on a different set of machinery, the initial costs of starting to manufacture are very great. They are also sometimes the result of the indivisibility of some large modern units of production, such as a steel mill or an oil refinery. Whatever the reason, the problems of embarking on industrial production are increased for the underdeveloped economy. Even if the necessary skill and capital can be found, production will not be economic unless the population is already rich enough to buy the new product on a large enough scale, or unless export markets can be guaranteed.

CONSUMPTION

The purpose of production is of course for use, and the process of using up commodities is known in economics as 'consumption'. In a sense, everything that is produced is eventually consumed, but in practice a distinction is normally drawn between production to satisfy the wants of consumers and production which is not directly for this purpose, which is most often production for investment. Consumers are directly concerned with the output of goods and services for immediate use, such as food, clothing, washing machines and motor cars, restaurants and television programmes. They are also concerned with some production for investment, such as housebuilding, although this kind of output can only be consumed slowly over a number of years. Other production for investment, such as machinery for making washing machines, or the building of a university which will produce teachers, doctors and other graduates whose services will one day be consumed, concerns consumers less directly, while the building of a steel mill or a chemical factory is even more remote to their interests. Most investment will however ultimately lead to the satisfaction of consumer wants, even though at many removes and often not for many years. The major exception (apart of course from unsuccessful investments) is expenditure on factories, machinery and skills for making armaments, just as the actual production of these can hardly be counted as raising an economy's standards of consumption.

A poor country with a low level and small range of production has naturally much less possibility of satisfying its consumers' wants than a rich one. But all countries have some choice as to how much production should be devoted to investment (and defence) and how much to consumption. It is in the pattern of consumption rather than of production that the main differences between the three groups of economies identified in the last chapter emerge. The governments of the communist countries do not allow the manufacture or import of consumer goods at the expense of capital goods for industry. Investment is given a higher priority than consumption, and industrial investment, being most likely to lead to economic growth, is given (together with defence) the highest priority of all. Wages are kept lower and the prices of consumer goods higher than in countries of similar national incomes per head, so that standards of living are in many respects lower. Consumers in some of these countries (or in some areas of them) benefit from certain items of high government investment expenditure, as on education or hospitals, but this is by no means general; in the USSR as a whole, for example, it is estimated that some 27 per cent of the age group 15–19 are in full-time secondary education, little more than in India, where the proportion is 22 per cent. (The proportion in the United States is 76 per cent.)

The pattern of consumers' expenditure in an underdeveloped country is distinguished by the very high proportion which is devoted to the basic necessities of life—food, clothing (although this varies with climate), and in urban communities housing. In the richer developed countries, after providing themselves with these necessities, consumers spend as much again on drink and tobacco, furniture, cars and electrical goods, or on services like holidays and cinemas. Despite the much larger and better quality diets of the inhabitants of developed countries (for example the average American gets through more than ten times the quantity of animal protein every day than the average Indian), there is a limit to the amount of food which can be eaten, and when a certain level of prosperity is reached the proportion of the average income spent on food begins to fall. This is also true to some extent of spending on clothing and housing.

The level and pattern of the average consumer's expenditure is always the most vivid illustration of economic life. From the two patterns of household expenditure compared in Table 2, all the main characteristics of the developed and the underdeveloped economy emerge. The low proportionate expenditure on food and the high level of spending on durable consumer goods and luxuries by the British household contrasts with the enormous proportionate expenditure on food and the tiny spending on everything else by the African household. The African family will have contributed a rather larger proportion of its income to taxes than appears here, since underdeveloped countries raise most of their revenue indirectly from taxes on imports or sales, which are then included in the prices charged to consumers. Nevertheless the taxes paid are still very small, as are savings. This shows how difficult it is for an underdeveloped country to accumulate capital for investment, or to provide the wide range of services to consumers that the British household enjoys and which do not appear in its expenditure—schools, medical services,

police, fire brigades, parks, good roads, museums and many other
things which contribute to standards of living.

TABLE 2
Two Patterns of Consumption

	Income and spending per household in Britain, 1965		Income and spending per African* household in Dar es Salaam, 1957	
	£	%	£	%
Food	327·6	19·5	49·3	51·9
Alcohol	80·6	4·8	1·0	1·1
Tobacco	80·6	4·8	3·8	4·0
Housing	139·4	8·3	7·2	7·6
Fuel and light	62·2	3·7	4·8	5·0
Clothing	115·9	6·9	3·3	3·3
Household goods	58·8	3·5 ⎫	0·7	0·7
Motor vehicles	45·4	2·7 ⎬		
Transport	42·0	2·5	1·5	1·6
Other	340·0†	20·3	20·2‡	23·4
Total spent	1292	77·0	93·6	98·6
Tax paid	297§	16·6	0·6	0·6
Saved	108	6·4	0·8	0·8
Total income	1680	100·0	95	100·0

* Dar es Salaam also has large Asian and European populations, whose
standards of living are higher. The African household in the capital
however has a higher standard of living than households in rural Tanzania.
† Largest items gambling (£22 per adult in 1965) and holidays.
‡ Largest item repayment of loans (£14·8). The British household also
lives on credit to some extent, but hire purchase repayments are included
in its spending on motor vehicles and other durable goods.
§ Including national insurance.

CHAPTER THREE

International Trade and Capital Movements

THE THEORY OF INTERNATIONAL TRADE

Although no country is entirely self-sufficient in the resources needed for modern economic life, some economies are very much better equipped than others. Such economies are relatively independent of international trade to maintain their standards of living. The USSR is one of these, producing over 95 per cent of the goods and services it uses itself, and the USA is another. In the less well endowed countries of Western Europe, on the other hand, at least 20 per cent of total national expenditure goes on imports. International trade does not, however, take place simply in commodities which one country can produce and another cannot, but mainly in commodities which one country can produce more cheaply or to a higher standard than another. One of the earliest preoccupations of economists was to explain why international trade takes place, what its value is to the economies concerned, and what the policy of governments should be towards it.

Nowadays economists spend little time on the general theoretical framework of international trade, but much on the particular trade problems of individual countries or groups of countries. In part this is a measure of the success of the classical doctrines of Adam Smith and David Ricardo, who developed this theory in the last quarter of the eighteenth century and the first quarter of the nineteenth. Their object was to demonstrate the gains from international trade. Today, these gains are largely taken for granted. In part, also, it must be admitted that the pattern of international trade has now become so complex and changes so rapidly that a satisfactory analysis of the gains to any two trading partners, particularly if they are developed countries, is very hard to make.

The early economists' statements on international trade are still worth reading today, among other reasons for the clarity and vigour of their expression, which is in marked contrast to the obscure jargon and arcane symbols of too many of their successors. For Adam Smith international trade was a means of enlarging the scope for the specialization and division of labour. 'It is the maxim of every prudent master of a family, never to attempt to make at home what it will cost him more to make than buy. The taylor does not attempt to make his own shoes, but buys them of the shoemaker. The shoemaker does not attempt to make his own clothes, but employs a taylor. The farmer attempts to make neither the one nor the other, but employs these different artificers. All of them find it for their interest to employ their whole industry in a way in which they have some advantage over their neighbours, and to purchase with a part of its produce, or what is the same thing, with the price of a part of it, whatever else they have occasion for.

'What is prudence in the conduct of every private family, can hardly be folly in that of a great kingdom. If a foreign country can supply us with a commodity cheaper than we ourselves can make it, better buy it of them with some part of the proceeds of our own industry, employed in a way in which we have some advantage. . . .

'The natural advantages which one country has over another in producing some commodities are sometimes so great, that it is acknowledged by all the world to be in vain to struggle with them. By means of glasses, hotbeds, and hotwalls, very good grapes can be raised in Scotland, and very good wine too can be made of them at about thirty times the expense for which at least equally good wine can be bought from foreign countries. Would it be a reasonable law to prohibit the importation of all foreign wines, merely to encourage the making of claret and burgundy in Scotland? But if there would be a manifest absurdity in turning towards any employment, thirty times more of the capital and industry of the country, than would be necessary to purchase from foreign countries an equal quantity of the commodities wanted, there must be an absurdity, though not altogether so glaring, yet exactly of the same kind, in turning towards any such employment a thirtieth, or even a three hundredth part more of either.'[1]

These ideas were greatly developed by David Ricardo. Smith had assumed that trade could only take place where each nation participating had an advantage over the rest in some particular line or lines. But what if there were countries which were unable to produce anything better or more cheaply than their neighbours? Ricardo developed the theory of comparative advantage to cover such a situation.

'Two men can both make shoes and hats, and one is superior to the other in both employments, but in making hats he can only exceed his competitor by one-fifth or 20 per cent, and in making shoes he can excel him by one-third or 33 per cent;—will it not be for the interest of both that the superior man should employ himself exclusively in making shoes and the inferior man in making hats.'[2]

The message of Ricardo's theory is the same as Smith's; governments should not set artificial barriers such as tariffs or other restrictions in the way of international trade. Such barriers, by limiting the extent of the market for the commodity in question, also limit the possibilities of specialization and hence of material progress for all concerned. The only possible exception to this general rule admitted by the classical economists was the 'infant industry' argument; a government might for a time be justified in maintaining trade barriers to protect a new industry, in which there was every prospect of a national advantage over other countries once well established. But for the greater part of the nineteenth century British industries were ahead of those of all other countries; free trade was wholly advantageous to Britain. The classical economists were therefore soon successful in altering British trade policy, and through Britain's economic leadership their ideas for a time dominated the world.

In real life, however, economic situations always were very

[1] *The Wealth of Nations*, Modern Library Edition, p. 424.
[2] *Principles of Political Economy*, Everyman's edition, p. 83. For an example worked out in modern terms see the appendix at the end of this chapter.

much more complex and confused than in the simple examples quoted, and in modern conditions their complexity has tended to increase. Knowledge of the data necessary to determine whether it would be better to produce one good rather than another is usually far from perfect, and the data themselves may moreover suddenly change, with an improvement in techniques or a change in consumers' tastes. Since their heyday in the middle of the nineteenth century free trade theories have wavered in popularity, suffering a particularly sharp decline during the great depression of the 1930's, to which they could offer no solution. Since the Second World War, there has been a revival, especially in Western industrialized countries, of interest in tariff cutting and trade liberalization as a means of stimulating production and increasing wealth. The formation of the European Common Market and the European Free Trade Area are the outstanding examples of this trend. The governments of the underdeveloped countries use import restrictions relatively freely, imposing quotas or tariffs with the object of protecting new industries, and also often using tariffs as a major source of revenue, since the poverty of their populations limits the other kinds of taxation open to them. Even these countries, however, have in recent years begun to try to establish freer trade between themselves; the Latin American Free Trade Area is the main example, but various African countries are investigating similar projects.

The governments of the communist countries, finally, pursue the most restrictive trade policies of all. This is a matter of political as well as economic policy, since they prefer to be independent of the rest of the world. It is also partly a matter of necessity, since they are usually extremely short of foreign exchange with which to pay for their imports. They normally allow imports only of commodities essential to achieving their long-term plans.

THE PATTERN OF INTERNATIONAL TRADE

Two countries whose trade with each other is high in relation to their outputs are said by economists to be 'complementary' to each other. The most obvious form of international complementarity is between an industrialized country and an agricultural one, the first importing from the second the raw materials and foodstuffs which it either cannot produce itself, or could only produce at much greater expense, and the second importing manufactures in exchange. During the last century international trade consisted mainly of such transactions, and world complementarity increased rapidly as the industrializing countries imported larger and larger quantities of raw materials and foodstuffs, and the primary producers imported the new manufactures—textiles and railway equipment were among the most important items. Even then, however, it would have been untrue to think of international trade as largely an exchange between these two sorts of economies, although it was largely an exchange of these two main types of commodity; the USA, which was itself a quickly industrializing country, was the main source of two important primary products for Europe, cotton and wheat. In this century, less and less international trade has been made up of the exchange of manufactures for primary products, and indeed international complementarity has never been so high as it was in 1913. More countries can produce their own manufactures, primary producers need a greater proportion of their output of foodstuffs to feed their own populations, synthetic substitutes have been developed for many raw materials that had once to be imported from where they were found, and there are more political barriers to trade. In the modern world the exchange of primary commodities for manufactures constitutes less than half of world trade, and since several primary products, such as wheat, cotton and tobacco, are exported by developed countries, the share of the underdeveloped countries in world trade is very much less than that.

Although international complementarity is not as high as it once was, world trade has nevertheless been growing rapidly in modern times. In 1964 the value of the world's exports was $168,650 million (£60,230 million), having more than doubled in a decade. This is roughly the equivalent of one year's production in the USA, and is about ten times what the whole of Africa produces in a year. Before discussing how the world total is shared between the three groups of economies, and the extent to which

TABLE 3
A Breakdown of World Exports, 1954 and 1964

	To developed countries		To underdeveloped countries		To Eastern bloc		To world	
	1954	1964	1954	1964	1954	1964	1954	1964
Developed countries								
$ million	35,505	85,045	14,960	24,305	1,160	4,600	52,160	114,710
% of total	68	74	29	21	2	4	100	100
Growth 1954–64 %	+140		+63		+297		+120	
Underdeveloped countries								
$ million	15,990	24,695	5,330	6,945	460	1,770	22,090	34,000
% of total	72	73	24	20	2	5	100	100
Growth 1954–64 %	+54		+30		+285		+54	
Eastern bloc								
$ million	1,288	3,880	472	2,630	6,690	13,090	8,600	19,940
% of total	15	19	5	13	78	66	100	100
Growth 1954–64 %	+201		+457		+96		+132	

Grand Total $ million   82,840   168,650

Note. The totals are slightly larger than the sum of the items due to exports classified to 'unknown' destinations.
Source: GATT.

each has participated in the overall growth, it is important to note the significance of foreign trade to the countries themselves. Of the three groups the underdeveloped countries are the most dependent on exports to maintain and increase their standards of living. With very few exceptions—India is one—they export well over 10 per cent of what they produce, and it is not difficult to find individual cases where the ratio is as high as one-third. Next come the developed countries, though there are considerable variations within this group. The communist countries are a long way behind, although some of them are now emerging quite rapidly from the Stalinist chrysalis of self-sufficiency.

The major part of world trade is, of course, accounted for by the developed countries, who were responsible for more than two-thirds in 1964. They have provided the main expansionary impetus, taking up more than 70 per cent of the total increase of $85,810 million between 1954 and 1964. More striking still is the fact that nearly 60 per cent of the total growth in world trade between these years was accounted for by the developed countries' trade with each other, an overwhelming proportion of this being manufactured goods. By 1964 the developed countries' trade with each other amounted to half the world total.

Part of the explanation for this must lie in the rapid growth of production, especially in Western Europe and Japan. However, the growth of the developed countries' trade with each other was twice as fast as the growth in their total ouput, and it is therefore clear that the removal of trade restrictions (notably the tariff cuts within the EEC[1] and the Japanese import liberalization programme[2]) has also played a part.

The limping growth of the underdeveloped countries presents a sad contrast to the booming exports of the developed. Between 1954 and 1964 exports by the underdeveloped countries rose by 54 per cent in comparison with the developed countries' 117 per cent. Indeed, the average achievement was even less if the Middle East, with its large petroleum resources, is excluded; the overall growth of exports by the remaining underdeveloped countries

[1] European Economic Community or European Common Market.
[2] Japan's imports rose more than threefold over the decade.

falls to 40 per cent. As a result of this trend there has of course been a sharp drop in the underdeveloped countries' share of world trade. At the same time, despite decolonization, their dependence on the markets of the developed countries has actually increased; nearly three-quarters of their exports went to these destinations in 1964. The problem for the underdeveloped world is that while the developed countries' demand for the products of other developed countries is growing much more rapidly than their total income, their demand for the exports of the underdeveloped countries is going up much more slowly than income. This is because the underdeveloped countries export mainly food and raw materials. At their present standards of living, most people in the developed countries do not choose to spend much of any increase in their incomes on food. At the same time, many of the industrial raw materials like rubber or cotton for which underdeveloped countries have natural climatic advantages can now be replaced by synthetic substitutes made in developed countries. Natural rubber, for example, now accounts for much less than half of total rubber consumption.

Exports by the communist economies have registered the fastest growth of all over the decade, rising by 132 per cent. The trading pattern has also been changing; in 1954 nearly 80 per cent of their trade was with each other, while ten years later this was down to one-third, exports to developed countries having tripled and those to underdeveloped countries having risen five and a half times. Nevertheless their share in world trade is still extremely small in relation to their population; their exports were only 12 per cent of world exports in 1964.

The most notable feature to emerge from this brief survey of world trade is the predicament of the underdeveloped countries. They are heavily dependent on exports to achieve higher incomes, and their exports are in turn heavily and increasingly dependent on finding markets in the developed countries. But the relationship is not reciprocal; the developed countries depend mainly on trading with each other, and this dependence is becoming more pronounced. The economic bargaining strength of the underdeveloped countries is therefore weak and seems to be becoming weaker. Nor is this the whole story, for there has also been a deterioration in the terms of trade of the underdeveloped countries, i.e. in the prices of their exports in relation to the prices of their imports. They have had to export a greater and greater volume to finance a given amount of imports, and it is estimated that this worsening in the terms of trade cost the underdeveloped countries around $4 billion in export earnings in 1954–64.[1] These are the problems which have faced most underdeveloped countries in recent years, and which underlie the accusations of 'neo-colonialism' which are levied against the developed world.

INTERNATIONAL CAPITAL MOVEMENTS

All countries both import and export goods, but only a few are significant exporters of capital. These are all among the developed countries of the West, led by the USA and the UK. International capital movements from these countries take many different forms. Private individuals invest in foreign countries by buying shares in foreign companies ('portfolio' investment), or transfer their funds to foreign banks for safer keeping or better interest rates. Companies make direct investments abroad by building factories or establishing mines or plantations, and also buy up the shares of foreign companies in order to own local subsidiaries. Governments and international organizations make foreign loans and grants, usually to other governments. Most of these and other forms of international capital movements are less well documented than is the case with international trade, and it is difficult to give a detailed description of the pattern as a whole.

In the present context, however, it is 'investment' capital from abroad that is of the greatest interest. The bulk of foreign investment capital is from private sources, and the pattern followed by these private funds is very similar to that of international trade. Developed countries supply most of the capital for export, and invest it mainly in each other. Table 4 shows the recent growth

[1] I. A. Maizels, *World Trade Problems and Trends of the 1960's.* Woolwich Economic Papers No. 7.

and distribution of private direct investment abroad by the USA, which is the world's largest capital source. Total US private direct investment abroad in 1964 exceeded the total exports of underdeveloped countries in that year by $10 billion (compare Tables 3 and 4).

TABLE 4

US Private Direct Investment Abroad in 1960 and 1964 ($ billion)

	In developed countries	In other countries	Total
1960	19·1	13·7	32·7
1964	27·9	16·0	44·3
Growth 1960–4 %	+46·0	+19·6	+35·0
Share of 1964 total %	63·0	37·0	100·0

+Source: *Survey of Current Business*. US Department of Commerce.

The table illustrates the main trend in the international flow of private capital, investment by developed countries in other developed countries. Big manufacturing concerns tend increasingly to establish or take over manufacturing facilities inside their previous export markets, and their export markets are mainly in other developed countries. In Britain in 1965 50 per cent of the value of the output of cars was from US-owned concerns, and 40 per cent of computers, petroleum and agricultural machinery; in France this was true of 20 per cent of petroleum and food, and over 40 per cent of the electronics industry. In West Germany 40 per cent of the motor industry was American-owned, and 80 per cent of computers. At the same time there were substantial West European assets in the USA, although they only amounted to some 12 per cent of US assets in Europe. European and American companies do, of course, invest in underdeveloped countries, particularly to develop valuable natural resources; nearly half of US investment in 'other countries' in 1964 was in mining and smelting and petroleum. To individual underdeveloped countries, indeed, the proportion of their total assets owned by foreigners often seems excessive, particularly as they themselves own nothing abroad. But their share of the new private capital available is nevertheless declining at a time when their shortage of capital is acute.

There is one very significant modification to this picture of the international flow of investment capital—international aid. This refers to certain capital flowing into the underdeveloped countries from the developed countries of the West, from the communist countries and from international institutions. The scale and growth of aid make up one of the most interesting international phenomena to have developed since the Second World War. In 1963, the latest year for which figures are available, total aid to underdeveloped countries was worth about $6·5 billion. A fuller account of this will be found in Part 2.

APPENDIX TO CHAPTER THREE

COMPARATIVE COSTS IN INTERNATIONAL TRADE

Consider first a situation where two countries, Britain and France, are each producing shoes.

	Annual output of shoes per worker
Britain	1,000
France	1,500

France clearly has an absolute advantage, and unless the British worker is prepared to accept much lower wages than his French counterpart or the British government takes steps to keep out French shoes, British shoemakers would soon be out of business.

Now suppose, due to a change in fashion, there is in both countries a sudden upsurge in the demand for hats, and the production possibilities are as follows:

	Annual output of shoes per worker	Annual output of hats per worker
Britain	1,000	1,600
France	1,500	2,000

Again France has the advantage. Does this mean that the British government has no alternative but to keep out both French hats and shoes in order to maintain employment in Britain? Ricardo showed that this does not follow. If France specializes in shoes and Britain in hats, then both countries will gain, and there will be more hats and shoes to satisfy the needs of both countries, *provided they trade with each other*. To follow this out with our example, what would happen if 4 British workers move from shoemaking to hat-making and 3 Frenchmen move in the other direction? In Britain the output of hats will rise at the expense of shoes, in France vice versa. In terms of our example the results of the change would be as follows:

	Change in annual output	
	shoes	*hats*
Britain: 4 workers move to hat-making	−4,000	+6,400
France: 3 workers move to shoemaking	+4,500	−6,000

The result of this redeployment of labour is that production of shoes rises by 500 and production of hats by 400. It is important to stress that these gains have been achieved without the need to add a single worker to either country's labour force.

Incidentally, this example illustrates one of the most fundamental economic concepts, that of *opportunity cost*. In simple terms this means looking at the costs of producing any commodity in terms of how the resources involved in its production might otherwise be employed. Thus, in our example, the opportunity cost for Britain in producing 6,400 hats is 4,000 shoes, while France is giving up the opportunity of producing 6,000 hats in order to make 4,500 shoes.

Ricardo's principle of comparative advantage can equally well be stated in terms of opportunity cost. In deciding to make hats instead of shoes, Britain is forfeiting less in terms of shoes forgone than would be the case if a similar decision were taken in France. (Britain would give up five-eighths of a shoe for each hat it produced, while France would give up one-eighth more, at three-quarters of a shoe, for the same result.) The opposite would be true if each country decided to specialize in making shoes; Britain would forfeit more than France. Thus the opportunity cost of making shoes is lowest in France and of hats in Britain. If each country specializes in the line in which its opportunity costs are lowest, both will gain.

PART TWO

THE EMERGENCE OF THE PRESENT STRUCTURE

The Nineteenth-Century Industrial Revolution

'He wished to know whether Hiram had seen fellows with staves and instruments spying about; they called themselves railroad people, but there was no telling what they were, or what they meant to do. The least they pretended was that they were going to cut Lowick parish into sixes and sevens.

'Why, there'll be no stirring from one pla-ce to another,' said Hiram, thinking of his wagon and horses.

'Not a bit,' said Mr. Solomon. 'And cutting up fine land such as this parish!—But there's no knowing what there is at the bottom of it. Traffick is what they put for'ard; but it's to do harm to the land and the poor man in the long run.'

(George Eliot, *Middlemarch*)

THE PROCESS OF INDUSTRIALIZATION

The emergence of the present world economic structure, with its great variations in national living standards, is a matter of the economic history of less than a hundred and fifty years. Britain was the first country to undergo the industrial revolution, but the agricultural labourers of *Middlemarch*, which is set in the early 1830's, from whose hay-forks the railway surveyors have to be rescued, led very similar lives to the peasants of many under-developed countries today. Existing on a few shillings a week, mostly illiterate, threatened by unemployment as a result of new farming methods, they had just begun to feel the impact of industrial society. The beginning of investment in the modern economy (the first public railway had opened in 1826) had done nothing so far to improve their standards of living, but was, as far

45

as most ordinary people were concerned, associated mainly with harder times. One of the greatest differences between the agricultural workers of early nineteenth-century England and those of Africa and Asia today must be in their attitudes to the changing scene. For the former, the new developments were suspicious, the new machinery a threat to employment; for the latter, the hopes of a better life are nearly always pinned to industrialization.

The industrial revolution began in Britain with the invention of machinery for textile production, operated first by water and later by steam power. Although the major inventions on which it was based—the spinning machine, the power loom, the use of coke for making pig iron, and the steam engine—were all developed during the eighteenth century, the process of economic reorganization took place in the nineteenth. This century saw the transformation of Britain from an agricultural to an industrial economy, and the transformation of British industry from the output of a limited number of skilled craftsmen, organized in units not usually much bigger than a household, into the mass production of factories and machines. At the beginning of the century, less than a third of the population of England and Wales lived in towns, and many of these lived in small towns with largely agricultural employment. By 1841 nearly half the population lived in towns, and by 1871 over 60 per cent; over these 70 years the population doubled.

The rate of change accelerated with the mechanization of transport. The new machinery could be used to full capacity once raw materials could be brought to the factories and finished products taken away as rapidly as manufacturing proceeded. Britain had 2,000 miles of railway by 1843, and 6,000 by 1850, and after 1850 steam began to replace sail for sea transport. Large-scale production based on steam power had spread by the middle of the century from cotton spinning to cotton and wool weaving, to the manufacture of machinery and iron and steel products, and was starting in many smaller industries. Growth was on a huge scale; the production of cotton cloth, for example, grew fivefold between 1820 and 1850, and the production of pig iron by nearly ten times. By the middle of the century, British exports were between two and three times as large as in 1800; by 1900 they were nearly seven times as large.

The industrialization of the other countries of Western Europe and of the USA was much slower to start, and for most of the century Britain remained well in the lead. In 1850 France had under 2,000 miles of railway and Germany had 3,600 miles; no other European country had as much as a thousand, and Russia only had 300. The USA however had 9,000 miles of track, which was rapidly opening up its western territories. British foreign trade was greater than that of France and Germany combined; British output of pig iron constituted half the world total, and Britain provided more than half the world's exports of manufactures. Even by the 1880's Britain was still producing nearly twice as much coal and pig iron as the USA, nearly three times as much of either as Germany, and France was still far behind. During the last decade of the century, however, the USA caught up. The enormous growth of the American population (from 13 million in 1830 to 76 million in 1900) and the prosperity of its agriculture built up a big market for manufactures, which American producers, partly with the help of protective tariffs, supplied themselves. Shortages of labour encouraged further improvements in machinery, and the next stage in technological innovation—the manufacture of consumer goods from interchangeable parts—was largely introduced in America for the production of sewing machines, bicycles, typewriters and clocks. By 1900 US pig iron production was well past Britain's; by 1910 it was three times as large. Germany, too, had begun to grow very quickly in the 1870's; German industry followed much the same pattern as British industry had done, but by then manufacturers were able to take advantage of many modern improvements. By the outbreak of the First World War German manufacturing production was slightly larger than the British.

Throughout the nineteenth century industrialization was accompanied by an enormous expansion in international trade. Britain, in the early stages of industrialization, imported increasing quantities of raw materials, particularly cotton, besides exporting increasing quantities of finished manufactures. As the industrial revolution progressed and the population increased the country ceased to be self-sufficient in food, as it had been more or less until this time. By 1875 nearly half of the British consumption of wheat and flour was imported, and imports of meat were beginning with the introduction of refrigeration. Local resources of iron ore were no longer enough to meet the iron industry's needs, and imports of wool and timber both rose even more rapidly in the second half of the century than the first. This pattern of expanding foreign trade was followed by the other industrializing European countries and later by the USA. The structure of American trade differed to some extent, however, as wheat was a major increasing export, and the USA remained a relatively self-sufficient economy; by 1913 the USA exported only some 8 per cent of its output and imported less. Britain exported nearly a quarter of its output, and imported nearly a fifth.

IMPROVEMENTS IN STANDARDS OF LIVING

An improvement in the standards of living of the European working classes was slow to follow industrialization. Increases in national output do not necessarily benefit the majority of a country's inhabitants. In Britain, it is estimated that national output approximately doubled between 1815 and 1850, but it is arguable whether the living conditions of the working classes improved at all. In many respects they grew worse; the agricultural labourers who were forced off the land by the enclosures drifted in search of work to industrial areas which were in no way equipped to receive a sudden increase of population. The village communities had given little more than a bare subsistence, and had ceased to do even that for many of their occupants, but socially they had provided far more than the conditions which prevailed in the miles of insanitary slum housing now hastily erected around the manufacturing towns. Contemporary descriptions, such as Engels' *Conditions of the Working Classes in England in 1844*, are their best illustration. Agriculture had on the whole provided regular employment, even in bad years; the industrial workers now found themselves frequently faced with temporary unemployment as a result of fluctuations in trade, and there were now no vegetable gardens, pigs and chickens to fall back on. Manufacturers, anxious to make the largest possible profits in order to build up the capital needed to expand their new ventures, kept wages to the minimum subsistence level, and exacted the longest possible hours of work. The exploitation of women and children was also on a scale unknown in agricultural employment.

By the middle of the century conditions were beginning to improve. National output nearly doubled again between 1850 and 1870, and this time a substantial proportion of the increase found its way to the working classes. A much more sophisticated financial system had developed with the expansion of the banks and the growth of joint stock companies. Manufacturers could now borrow money more easily to cover their short-term needs, and could raise long-term capital from shareholders. This reduced the pressure to keep wages down, and in the 1850's the workers in manufacturing industry became substantially better off than the 20 per cent of the labour force who remained on the land. Food prices had become relatively stable; the repeal of the Corn Laws in 1847 meant that the British consumer could benefit from cheap imports of wheat and flour, and in the 1870's still cheaper grain began to arrive from the USA. Although this meant depression in agriculture, for workers in industry wages either rose or fell less rapidly than prices, for the rest of the century. Average real wages, i.e. wages allowing for changes in prices, approximately doubled between 1860 and 1896; the improvement in the standards of living of skilled workers in manufacturing industry was much greater, and they began to enjoy a way of life that had previously been reserved for the middle classes. But for other employees the improvement was less; for agricultural labourers in many areas there was none, and there was no provision outside the workhouse for the old until 1908 or any of the unemployed until 1911. One of the first sociological surveys, carried out by B. S. Rowntree in York in 1901, showed that 28 per cent of the population were living in households whose incomes were below what had been estimated as a minimum subsistence level. Moreover, in the years leading up to the First World War prices rose faster than wages, and real wages consequently declined; average real earnings in 1913 were a little below those of 1895.

In Britain in 1913, the earnings of an agricultural labourer averaged 17s. a week; a man employed in manufacturing averaged £1 12s. Average male earnings in manufacturing in Britain in 1964 were over £18 a week, but prices rose more than 500 per cent over the fifty years, so that the earnings of 1913 were worth something more like £8 in modern terms. Wages in the USA were higher than in Britain before the industrial revolution began, and they remained ahead. The prosperity of American agriculture and the constant opening up of new land provided competition to industrial employment, and labour remained in short supply in the manufacturing areas despite the immigration of millions of Europeans. At the outbreak of war, average real income per head in America was about 20 per cent higher than in Britain. France and Germany were still on average poorer than Britain, as they had been throughout the century, and they both continued to have larger agricultural populations. German incomes have been estimated at a little more than 70 per cent of the British, and French incomes at about 65 per cent.

By the outbreak of the First World War, much of the economic structure of the modern world had become apparent. The USA, the UK and Germany were the leading industrial powers; France was also by most definitions a developed country, although it had not yet entered the age of mass production, specializing rather in small-scale skilled manufacturing and remaining self-sufficient in agriculture. Russian industrialization was still very limited, and heavily dependent on foreign technicians, but the Russian railway system was now larger than any other except the American, and Russian pig iron was beginning to catch up with the French. Australia was prosperous on wool and wheat, and Japan had just become a net exporter of manufactures. The steady growth in the national products of the industrializing powers was a new economic phenomenon, unknown in the old world of primary producers. It meant that by about 1870 the national products of the UK, USA, France and Germany, with populations measured in tens of millions, were approaching the same order of magnitude as the products of India and China, with

populations measured in hundreds of millions. By 1913 the great
gap between the average incomes per head in the USA, Canada,
Britain, Australia, Germany and France, and in the countries of
Asia, Africa and South America, was already a fact, although it
was to grow far wider still.

CHAPTER FIVE

The Role of Governments in Western Industrialization

THE THEORY OF LAISSEZ FAIRE

In seventeenth-century France the minister Colbert asked a merchant what the government should do to encourage trade. Numerous medieval restrictions and taxes on trade and industry were still in force, and the first half of the famous reply, 'Laissez faire et laissez passer', can be freely translated as 'Leave us alone to get on with it.' Colbert, while reforming the old system, was in fact responsible for a major extension of government regulation and control over economic affairs, and it was not until two centuries later, and in England, that the merchant's advice was taken. The phrase came to stand for the theories of the 'classical' British economists, which dominated British government policy in the nineteenth century, and had a wider international influence for longer still.

The basic theme of laissez faire economics is extremely simple to grasp, which must account for some of its success. It is that if every man is free to make the most money he can, with no government interference either to obstruct or protect him, the largest possible income must accrue to the country as a whole. It implies that the government's proper role in the economy is a minimal one; its functions should be limited to the maintenance of law, order and defence, and taxes should be levied only to cover the cost of these operations. The theory extends to international economic relations: governments should not interfere with foreign trade by imposing tariffs or other restrictions on imports or exports, because if each country exports as much as possible of what it can produce most cheaply, and imports the cheapest products of others, the incomes of all countries will be maximized.

The main assumption underlying laissez faire economic theories is that all individuals are equally able to choose their occupations, to change to those in which earnings are higher, and to save enough to become capital owners on their own account. These conditions have been more nearly fulfilled in certain countries and at certain times than others; they were certainly very far from true in nineteenth-century England. Nor are they true, although more nearly so, of modern America and Canada, where laissez faire theories developed later and survived more generally than elsewhere. However, modern proponents of these theories still argue against government action to modify inequalities of wealth on the grounds that riches have been acquired as a result of individual enterprise and hard work (and that one of the rewards of this is to leave one's children well provided for), while poverty must conversely be to some extent the result of lack of effort by the poor.

In Britain, the application of the theories of free enterprise and free trade coincided with the industrial revolution. Production boomed, standards of living rose, and the number of capital owners increased rapidly. British exports, in demand all over the world, had as yet no serious competition, while at home manufacturers benefitted from being able to import raw materials free of duty, and the industrial working classes from cheap imported food. The validity of laissez faire theories seemed, at least to the new capitalist class, to be amply confirmed. In America, on the other hand, the industrial revolution was carried out without the adoption of free trade, and in its early stages there was even positive government intervention at home. Several State governments took an active part in economic development, operating railways, canals, banks and many other concerns. Towards the end of the century, however, private capital became more generally available for development, and discredit was brought on various state enterprises through inefficient management by politicians. (Officials were changed, as is still the American system in the upper ranks of administration, with changes in government.) Public opinion swung in favour of private enterprise, and since its expansion coincided with a phenomenal growth in American production, fresh glamour was shed on the concept of laissez faire.

THE EROSION OF LAISSEZ FAIRE

Government intervention in economic life can be broadly speaking of two kinds. A government can intervene positively, for example by using the taxpayers' money to make investments and by running industrial and commercial concerns itself. It can also intervene restrictively (though normally with a positive object in doing so), for example by making rules about wages and working conditions, by requiring industry to be located in specified areas, or by deciding that some industries should be encouraged and others held back. During the nineteenth century, a wide range of new products could still be invented, perfected and put into production at the cost of relatively small amounts of capital, which individual businessmen could raise themselves. As the nineteenth-century industrial revolution gathered momentum, the modern system of ownership of enterprises by companies with several shareholders was evolved, which provided private capital on a much larger scale. There was therefore no obvious need for the government concerned to play a positive role in economic development by mobilizing capital, although there are other forms of positive intervention which could have been valuable. In Germany, for example, the government made a substantial investment in technical education, which was to prove very useful to the economy.

In the early stages of industrial revolution in Britain and America there was also virtually no restrictive government intervention, and since most government controls, whatever their intention, tend to be somewhat clumsy in their application, this probably contributed to the speed of innovation. The incidental expense, in terms of the sufferings of the working classes, was according to classical economic theory unavoidable. The classical theory of wages was the 'iron law'—that employers must in the long run pay the minimum wage necessary for subsistence. If they pay less, starvation reduces the labour force, so that wages rise again; if they pay more, the population increases and unemployment drags wages down. Any government interference with wages or working conditions is therefore useless as well as undesirable.

In nineteenth-century England the existence of a social and economic order involving wide disparities of income was hardly as yet questioned, but the situation of the new industrial working class led very early to a clash between humanitarian views, which demanded government intervention, and economic theories, which opposed it. The first achievements of the humanitarians, the early Factory Acts, were mainly aimed at the regulation of child labour, and children could hardly be argued to be individuals able to make a free choice for themselves. The legislation was nevertheless considered at the time to be economically unsound. From the middle of the century, government regulation of hours and conditions of work became more general, but the passage of the various Acts by which this was achieved was the result of largely emotional argument; the national success of laissez faire was too great for any rival theory to be seriously considered. The tiny minorities who were already involved with Christian Socialism in England, or who took an interest in the views of the Utopian Socialists in France, or who absorbed Marxist ideas and joined the Social Democratic party in Germany, still had no influence on governments.

By the end of the century, however, the political climate was changing. All countries except Britain and the Netherlands had abandoned laissez faire economic policies, and even in Britain a substantial body of opinion was pressing for free trade to be abandoned. In the search for new markets, the European powers had all expanded their colonies overseas; government intervention and support had always in the end proved necessary, even where private traders had first opened up the new territory. In Germany, Britain's major European rival, a late industrial revolution had taken place under a system of relatively close State regulation; the German success had done much to revive the idea of positive government intervention in the domestic economy. The spread of socialist ideas, both as Marxism and in the more liberal form represented by the Fabians in England, had begun to worry and to influence governments. Working-class interests had begun to organize, against a background, in most of Northern Europe and America, of almost universal male suffrage. In Britain the membership of trade unions affiliated to the TUC in 1885 was 0·5 million; by 1900 it was 1·2 million and two Labour members were returned to Parliament; by 1914 membership had reached 4 million.

By 1914 the role of governments, particularly in Europe, was considerably greater than the economists of a hundred years earlier would have considered desirable. Government restrictions on economic freedom were general, and a small degree of positive intervention had crept in. Hours and conditions of work were regulated to a large extent, and this had not proved economically disastrous. National insurance schemes, pioneered by Germany, although by no means comprehensive and on a very modest scale, protected certain categories of workers against sickness and unemployment in several European countries and in New Zealand. In Germany, old age pensions had been introduced in 1889; Britain followed in 1908, and in 1909 the British government began to operate labour exchanges. State primary education was free and compulsory. The erosion of laissez faire had begun, though it was still on a small scale. A mixture of humanitarian motives, the problems of large urban populations at home and colonies abroad, and the haphazard requirements of other economic pressure groups had enforced some enlargement of the economic role of governments, but it took the catastrophe of the First World War to reveal how big a part this was to be.

THE 1914-1918 WAR

'Men are reluctant to believe that great events have small causes,' A. J. P. Taylor observes in his history of the First World War,[1] and in attempts to explain the war economic forces are often argued to have been at work. In fact economic causes were largely absent. The tariff barriers which had been rising over most of Europe since the end of the nineteenth century were signs of growing nationalism, but not contributions to it; Germany's territorial ambitions in Europe and all the great powers' rival colonial intentions in Africa and the Middle East were not

[1] A. J. P. Taylor, *The First World War*, Hamish Hamilton, 1963.

related to pressing economic needs, though the potential profits were of course attractive. Germany and Britain were indeed economic rivals, producing a very similar range of manufactures for much the same markets. German efficiency, particularly in the iron and steel and engineering industries, tended to be greater than in the longer established British equivalents; German technical and scientific education was on an appreciably larger scale. Germany was a high tariff country, whereas Britain maintained free trade, and German exports were even providing serious competition for some British goods at home. However, this situation was not new; German competition had been of far greater concern to British manufacturers in the early 1880's, when trade in general was depressed and Britain was not accustomed to economic rivalry. Nor was this a cause for war, any more than it is today, and indeed contemporary observations on the different approaches of the two powers to exporting sound very familiar in the context of the 1960's; the Germans' readiness to learn foreign languages, their greater attention to individual customers' requirements and their willingness to arrange long credit periods were all being quoted against the British eighty years ago.

If the Great War was short of economic causes, however, its economic consequences were many, although most of those concerned with the peace negotiations failed to realize this. 'To what a different future Europe might have looked forward, if either Mr. Lloyd George or Mr. Wilson had apprehended that the most serious of the problems which claimed their attention were not political or territorial but financial and economic,' J. M. Keynes, who was present at the negotiations as a British Treasury representative, wrote afterwards (and after resigning) in his *Economic Consequences of the Peace*. President Wilson had indeed included the removal of economic barriers to trade in the original 'fourteen points' of his proposal to end the war in 1917, but the peace settlement of 1919, with its establishment of a number of new independent states in Europe, in fact split up areas of free trade and increased tariff walls. International trade was already distorted by the war. The European powers had been largely cut off from their overseas markets for four years; in many of these, especially Japan, India and Argentina, local producers had taken the opportunity to substitute domestic manufactures. At the same time the demands of the war had led to greatly increased production of primary commodities—food and raw materials—in any area from which supplies could be obtained. As a result there was now a problem of over-production, especially for wheat, sugar, coffee and rubber; the prices of primary products fell, and primary producing countries imported less. But the chaotic state of prices and currencies constituted for the moment a still worse setback to trade. Before the war, currencies had been freely convertible into gold, which meant that the banks of the economy concerned would always exchange its currency notes for gold at a fixed rate. The war had caused most countries to abandon the gold standard, so that prices in the different countries were free to move independently. Prices had risen rapidly during the war years, at rates varying with the extent of government control over the economy, and the post-war inflation was much worse; the German, Russian and Austro-Hungarian currencies all became virtually worthless; in Britain prices rose till 1920, when they were three times the level of 1913, while in France prices went on rising till 1926, to reach a peak of eight times their pre-war level.

The cost of the war to the British Exchequer had been some £9,000 million; the cost in other terms was some three-quarter million dead, but there had been little civilian damage except to merchant shipping. The war had indeed stimulated growth in certain sectors. Destruction in Europe was also on a small scale compared to what was to be brought about by the Second World War, but the cost in death was far worse—nearly one and a half million each for France and Germany, and Russian losses of probably more than all the rest put together. The USA suffered no economic setbacks, but 88,000 dead. The war had, however, left a complicated structure of international debt. Britain had lent her allies, including Russia, now in the midst of revolution, over £1,800 million (the equivalent of about half the national income for 1913). Italy, Belgium and France were in debt to each other as well as to Britain, and Britain owed the USA over £1,000 million.

British and French public opinion called for Germany to bear the full cost of the war, for the Allied governments to 'squeeze the lemon till the pips squeak' in the unpleasant phrase of Sir Eric Geddes. In a world in which economic processes were still very little understood, many of the politicians and civil servants concerned were unable to see that for Germany to amass and transfer reparations on the scale they were demanding would be likely to damage their own economies. If Germany made reparations in the form of gold and foreign exchange, she could only earn these by exporting more than she imported, which would be at the expense of the Allies' export markets; if reparations were made in the form of German goods, the inflow of these would again be at the expense of domestic industries. In any case in 1919 Germany had nothing left with which to start payment. Lloyd George was aware of the impractical nature of the demands for reparations, but was not prepared to stand up to public opinion. His solution was to allow Germany to be saddled by the peace treaty with an enormous reparations obligation, while fully realizing that she would never pay it. This was to have unfortunate consequences for the restoration of confidence in the German economy, and for international relations.

The legacies of the First World War to the world economy were distorted production and trade, high tariffs, weak currencies and international indebtedness. On a national scale, the European governments were left a more useful economic inheritance, which was the demonstration of the feasibility of major positive government intervention in an industrialized economy. The giant scale of mobilization, with millions employed in the manufacture of armaments as well as in the armed forces, made central direction essential. In Britain, with hardly any official change in policy (although some anti-free traders joined the government when the Coalition was formed in 1916), the government found itself exercising almost every possible form of economic power. Labour was directed to where it was required; industries were enlarged or reduced by means of government allocation of raw materials, itself based on import controls; the railways and the mines were nationalized, and government monopolies bought and sold wheat and sugar. By the end of the war food was rationed and the government was exercising an important influence on wage levels through what it paid its own employees.

'War socialism', as Churchill called it, was a haphazard development of ad hoc solutions to war needs. It did not include any long term central planning; the new controls were expected to be temporary, and indeed although statutory powers lay behind them the wartime ministries were largely able to operate with the voluntary co-operation of shopkeepers and factory owners. While displacing laissez faire, war socialism did not stand for any new economic theory. Socialism itself, originally strongly internationalist in outlook, had received a severe blow from the outbreak of war; many continental socialist leaders had believed until the fighting actually started that the working classes would refuse to take up arms against each other. Nevertheless, war socialism had shown that a government could play a major part in the direction and control of a modern economy without economic disaster. Many private enterprises had indeed made large profits by co-operating with the government, while for the working classes the war years were associated with full employment and, at least towards the end, rising standards of living. The British government dismantled nearly all its economic apparatus in the two or three years after the war. But the age of laissez faire was in fact over; it was no longer possible for the industrialized countries to continue to increase production, exports and standards of living without government control and support, and international co-operation between governments. A rival economic system was in the process of being set up in Russia, although the Western powers still expected the Bolshevik régime to prove a temporary phenomenon. The death struggles of laissez faire had, however, to continue for another twenty years, while the governments of the developed countries made up their minds to assume new responsibilities.

CHAPTER SIX

The Communist Economies and Industrialization

MARXISM

In 1917 the Bolsheviks took control of the Russian Revolution and began to establish the first Communist state. To most foreign observers, it seemed improbable that their régime would last. They were engaged in civil war not only with the White Russian forces, but also soon with other socialists, and in July 1918 the Allied forces began to intervene, in principle to re-establish an eastern front against the Germans, but hoping incidentally to overthrow the Bolsheviks as well. However, while Russia at the end of the First World War contained about 8 per cent of the world's population, the population of the communist economies today constitutes about one-third. Not only did the Bolsheviks retain power in Russia, but they succeeded, partly by conquest, but also by inspiration, in spreading their form of government throughout Eastern Europe and China.

Communist states are governed in principle according to Marxist theory, although in practice there has always been considerable deviation from what Marx actually predicted or taught. Marx's economic, historical and sociological theories are interdependent; they unite to claim that past and future developments in economic and social life follow an inevitable pattern, which may be understood through a study of Marx's work. Marxism is in this sense a religion; Marxist ideas began indeed to spread at a time when a period of Christian revival was drawing to a close. Schumpeter, an economist who believed firmly in private enterprise but who was a great admirer of Marx, analysed Marx's success in offering a new religion by 'weaving together those extra-rational cravings which receding religion had left running about like masterless dogs, and the rationalistic and materialistic

61

tendencies of the time—which would not tolerate any creed that had no scientific or pseudo-scientific connotation. Preaching the goal would have been ineffectual; analysing a social process would have interested only a few hundred specialists. But preaching in the garb of analysis and analysing with a view to heartfelt needs, this is what conquered passionate allegiance and gave to the Marxist that supreme boon which consists in the conviction that what one is and stands for can never be defeated but must conquer victoriously in the end.'[1] It is necessary to remember that Marxism contains this religious element, unmatched in Western economic theories except perhaps by a few eccentric exponents of extreme laissez faire. Economic decisions by communist governments which evidently have disastrous short-term consequences, and whose long-term effects seem at best very doubtful, are only explicable in the light of Marxist faith.

Marxist theory states that any society must in the course of history move through a series of preordained states, before it finally attains the ideal of communism, when in a situation of economic abundance society will—in Marx's famous phrase—'inscribe upon its banners: from each according to his ability, to each according to his needs'. This theory is based on Marx's 'economic interpretation' of history; his historical research purported to show that the kind of society which has existed at any time and in any country has been fundamentally determined by economic conditions. His main illustrations are the 'handmill' and 'steam mill' societies; the handmill form of production is said to provide the basis for a feudal society, while the steam mill, requiring a large sum of investment, calls into being the capitalist society controlled by the middle classes or bourgeoisie. Each form of production contains within itself the factors which will give rise to the next form; in the handmill society, machines will inevitably sooner or later be invented, while in the capitalist society the exploitation of the proletariat, who own nothing, by the capitalists who own the means of production, will eventually lead to its destruction. Marx believed, with earlier economists such as Ricardo, that the value of any commodity depends on the

[1] J. A. Schumpeter, *Ten Great Economists from Marx to Keynes*, New York, OUP, 1951.

quantity of labour required to produce it, as measured in hours of work. This is an untenable assumption, but it is basic to his 'theory of exploitation', which explains the inevitability of class war. The value of the labourer's work, like that of any other commodity, is said to depend on the number of hours' work which went to feed and otherwise enable him to survive to adult life, and which are necessary for him to subsist now. The capitalist will pay him the value of these hours (i.e. the subsistence wage of the 'iron law'). But the labourer actually works for far more hours than these, so 'surplus value' goes to the capitalist, who accumulates most of it in the form of more and more capital. This he will use to build more and larger factories, using increasing amounts of machinery. Eventually far more commodities will be produced than can be sold, since the capitalists' own wants will be satisfied, and the working classes have not the means to buy them. Economic chaos will follow, and the increasing misery of the proletariat, thrown out of work first by mechanization and then by factory closures, will lead to revolution. Marx's description of this stage comes in Chapter XXXII of *Das Kapital*: 'Along with the constantly diminishing number of the magnates of capital, who usurp and monopolize all advantages of this process of transformation, grows the mass of misery, oppression, slavery, degradation, exploitation: but with this too grows the revolt of the working class, a class always increasing in numbers, and disciplined, united by the very mechanism of the process of capitalist production itself. The monopoly of capital becomes a fetter upon the mode of production. . . . Centralization of the means of production and socialization of labour at last reach a point where they become incompatible with their capitalist integument. This integument bursts. The knell of capitalist private property sounds. The expropriators are expropriated.'

The post-revolutionary stage of society, 'the dictatorship of the proletariat', is the stage of socialism. All communist states now classify themselves as being in this stage, which is the preliminary to achieving the ideal communist society. The workers are in control, but production has not yet been increased to a level at which there is enough of everything for everybody to have what they need. The workers must therefore operate a system of government, whereas when communism can be introduced the state will 'wither away'. Marx did not give detailed indications of the characteristics of the socialist society. He did, however, advocate the nationalization of all means of production, equal pay for everybody, and—most important of all—planning, in order to replace the chaos of capitalism and to increase production as rapidly as possible.

The various communist countries have evolved their own forms of the socialist society, and have frequently altered these. The nationalization of the means of production has nearly always been a factor, and equal pay has sometimes been tried, but the outstanding characteristic which distinguished the communist from the Western economies, at least until the second half of this century, has been the communist emphasis on central planning and the determination to maintain at any cost a high rate of economic growth. This is based on investment in the means of production, i.e. mainly in heavy industry, which has been promoted in all communist countries at the expense of industries producing consumer goods and of agriculture.

COMMUNISM IN RUSSIA

On the outbreak of the First World War, Russia was still a largely peasant society, with only 10 per cent of the labour force employed in industry and an estimated 20 per cent of the population literate. National income per head was perhaps one-sixth what it was in Britain. Russia was, however, well into the stage of economic 'take off', and had been developing particularly fast in the years immediately before the war; industrial production had increased by well over 50 per cent between 1909 and 1913. There were substantial metallurgical, textile and mining industries, and because these had developed later than elsewhere they had relatively modern equipment. Industry was organized into unusually large—for that date—manufacturing units, and this, besides being more economic, was to assist the political organization of industrial workers. But Russian industry had been very largely developed by foreign interests; in 1913 over 40 per cent of shares in limited companies were owned by foreigners, and there were many foreign managers and technicians in Russian industry. It has been estimated that half the coal industry and over half of pig iron production was controlled by French companies and share-holders, and German, British and Belgian interests were also substantial.

The rapid growth of the pre-war years, together with the beginnings of liberalization of the Tzarist régime, seemed to indicate that Russia was likely to become a constitutional monarchy at the same time as a great industrial power, or, in Marxist terms, to be entering the capitalist stage of its economic history, in which the bourgeoisie would be in control. The revo-lution of February 1917 was a surprise to all political parties. It was the result of the sufferings brought about by the war, to which Russian economic resources had been devoted on a huge scale. The drafting of peasants into the army sharply reduced the output of food and the breakdown of the railways brought large towns near to starvation. When the Provisional Government of liberals allied with progressive right-wing politicians was set up, the Bolsheviks among the other Marxist socialists believed that a long period of middle-class democratic government had begun. In April, however, Lenin returned from exile and astonished his followers with the announcement that the time had already come to take power. In October, the Bolshevik 'Red Guards' rose in Petrograd and arrested the members of the Provisional Govern-ment. In November the Constituent Assembly was elected, the Bolsheviks winning only a quarter of the votes. When the Assem-bly met early in 1918 and refused to vote itself out of power, the Red Guards shut out the delegates and fired on demonstrators. The Bolsheviks—the name of the party was shortly afterwards changed to the Communist Party—were from then on in control, a situation which they maintained first by eliminating their main political opponents and later by purging their own ranks.

The Bolsheviks therefore took control of a situation quite unlike any described by Marx. There was no great industrial proletariat united in demanding the overthrow of capitalism; on the contrary the most numerous workers were peasants whose great desire was to own their own land. There had been no previous stage of over-production, indeed output of everything except armaments was almost at a standstill. Not only was the country engaged in war with Germany, but the Bolsheviks were soon faced with civil war against both right- and left-wing opponents. In the chaos of the first years of the revolution, the economic measures taken to establish socialism were largely a matter of haphazard improvisation by the central government, and of steps taken by local revolutionary leaders who were at first relatively free from central control.

The first few steps taken by the Bolsheviks to socialize the Russian economy included the nationalization of land. The peasants in many areas had already divided up the big estates among themselves, so this was only a legalization of the existing situation. A few big farms were kept as state farms. Banks, railways and other large concerns were nationalized, and 'workers' councils' were elected in all enterprises to supervise production— in many cases, particularly the railways, with chaotic results. Equal pay was introduced, at least in theory. But ordinary market relationships were still supposed to exist between firms, whether publicly or privately owned, and it was still hoped to attract foreign capital.

After the civil war broke out, it was felt that capitalists could no longer be allowed to have any influence over economic affairs, since they might attempt to sabotage the communist war effort. Everything was therefore nationalized, except agriculture, and a system was introduced which was later labelled 'war communism', although at the time it was thought of as a permanent reform. Trade having also been nationalized, private exchanges of any sort were forbidden; the peasants were required to deliver their food to the co-operatives and food supply organizations in the towns in exchange for manufactures. Since industry was still hardly functioning, there were few manufactures to exchange, so the peasants kept their wheat until it was forcibly taken from them. It was hoped to do away with money altogether; wages were paid in kind where possible, and public services in so far as they still existed were free. Government economic planning began, in that production orders were given to each enterprise, but these were not co-ordinated with each other nor with the availability of raw materials. Exchanges between enterprises were further complicated by the decision not to use money; bartering agreements had to be made, usually on a quite irrational basis.

Russian war communism was an attempt to introduce Marx's ideal communist society in conditions of general want, deprivation and economic disorder, instead of waiting for the state of total abundance which he had assumed to be its basis. Its economic consequences were disastrous, although it is hard to distinguish these from the destruction caused by the German and civil wars. In 1921, when the civil war ended, Russian industrial output was at about 14 per cent of its 1913 level. Agricultural output was about half; iron and steel production had almost stopped, as had railway traffic. There was bitter discontent among the peasants because of the continued state confiscation of their crops without payment, and also among the industrial proletariat, although the numbers of this class had fallen to little over a million as the workers had left the towns in search of food. Such economic life as still existed depended mainly on black market activities.

It was evident to Lenin that private enterprise would have to be restored to some extent in order to save the situation. In 1921 he introduced his 'new economic policy' (NEP). The peasants were to pay a fixed tax in food instead of the arbitrary quotas; private retail trade was restored so that they could sell their surplus output for whatever prices they could get. It became legal to rent land or hire labour; small manufacturing enterprises were denationalized and foreign and bourgeois specialists were re-employed as necessary. Equal pay was abandoned, and cash wages and even union bargaining was restored. Money assumed its old role to a large extent; nationalized enterprises had to pay each other for goods and services received. The mixture of public and private enterprise in the USSR then was not unlike the situation in the UK today, although the banks, foreign trade and all large industrial enterprises were nationalized and there was of course far more direct state interference with production. State planning under the NEP was also similar to current British practice; the planners calculated future production figures as targets, not as orders; they could not control sales, as a high proportion were always to the private sector, and they were mainly concerned with planning the pattern of investment. Much experimental work on planning and growth was done by Soviet economists at this time. The economic freedoms granted under the NEP lasted essentially unchanged for seven years, although much encouragement was given during this time to the expansion of trading co-operatives and state farms. Despite the setback of two terrible years of drought, which spread famine over wide areas of the country (when the American Relief Association was allowed in to distribute food and medicine), pre-war levels of production in industry and agriculture had largely been achieved by 1927. But the NEP, although successful, fitted into no Marxist category. Private enterprise was an important feature of the economy, but it was allowed no political power; economic conditions plainly did not dictate the form of society, but the politicians decided the form of the economy. The Soviet solution was not to give the capitalists political representation, but once again to put an end to capitalism.

Lenin died in 1924, but the end of the NEP and the period of Stalinism really began in 1928 with the introduction of the First Five Year Plan. The concept of a Five Year Plan was considered in the West to be one of the most striking developments in the USSR, but in fact Soviet planning had been very much more constructive before it was introduced. Industry was now re-nationalized, together with most of trade. Direct physical planning of production was restored; industries and enterprises were now ordered to reach stated levels of production in each year. The emphasis was on heavy industry (which was allocated nearly 80 per cent of all investment in the First Five Year Plan), and the targets almost arbitrarily chosen. The 90 per cent of agriculture which remained outside the state farms was now forcibly organized into collective farms, although small private plots were eventually allowed. The rest of the private sector was limited to trade in second-hand goods, domestic service and the building of small houses, with a little private education and medicine. The system differed from war communism mainly in that money was retained in its normal role; enterprises had to pay each other and so to keep separate accounts and to be relatively cost-conscious, and consumers, being paid in money, could to some extent refuse to buy unwanted commodities. However from 1928 onwards the government decided all changes in prices, and as time went on these became more and more peculiar in relation to each other. The economic consequences of Stalinism for agriculture were grave; the social consequences were tragic. The peasants' resistance to collectivization and the low level of investment directed to agriculture combined to produce a drop in cereal production over the five years of the First Plan, and a sharp decline in the numbers of livestock, which the peasants often decided to eat rather than hand over to the collective. The responsibility for agricultural failure was attributed to the rich peasants or kulaks, a definition which was widely extended (the kulaks had been estimated to own under 5 per cent of farms in 1928). The extension of collectivization was combined with the policy of 'elimination of kulaks as a class', and the local executive committees were soon given the right to confiscate the kulaks' goods and expel them from the district. In 1932 the death penalty was introduced for 'damaging collective property'. Thousand of peasants were deported to labour camps, and thousands more died of starvation while the land remained uncultivated. Collectivization was completed under the Second Five Year Plan, and agricultural output then began to grow again, though slowly. Part of its continuing troubles, after the open resistance to collectivization was over, were due to the government's pricing policy; the prices for the compulsory deliveries to the state by the collectives were fixed at the 1928 levels amid a general inflation.

The growth rates claimed for heavy industry under Stalinism were invariably spectacular, though since most industries were being built up from almost nothing, and since they received the lion's share of investment, they could be expected to be high. Moreover Soviet production figures have to be treated with some caution, as a result of the unpleasant personal consequences to managers of not fulfilling targets, at least on paper. One obvious way out, particularly in consumer goods industries, was to abandon quality. But progress was undoubtedly rapid. The Russians claim that the output of heavy industry increased by over 270 per cent in 1928/32, and by well over 100 per cent in 1933/37, and that during the second period consumers' expenditure almost doubled. It is difficult to estimate the level of incomes or standards of living in communist countries (see Chapter 1), but it has been calculated that at the outbreak of the Second World War income per head in the USSR was about one third of what it was in the UK.

POST-WAR COMMUNIST SYSTEMS

The Second World War caused fearful destruction in the painfully built up Soviet economy. The USSR suffered more from German invasion than any other country. The war nevertheless enabled the Russians to assist or impose the establishment of other communist régimes in the countries of Eastern Europe which the Red Army liberated at the end of the war—Rumania, Bulgaria, Hungary, Yugoslavia, Czechoslovakia, Poland and finally East Germany.

The communist régimes which were established in these countries were replicas of the Stalinist model in the USSR. They were further handicapped by very disadvantageous 'trade agreements', or war reparations, imposed by Russia; raw materials and manufactures were supplied by the satellite countries to the Soviet Union in large quantities for several years after the war, in exchange for little or nothing. Their economic development was therefore geared to Russian needs rather than to their own, in so far as needs were considered. In general the Plans for these countries were based on the Soviet assumption that heavy industry must be developed at all costs.

It was, however, in one of these satellites—Yugoslavia—that the first major development in communist economics since 1928 appeared. Marshal Tito broke with Stalin in 1948, and over the next few years dismantled nearly all the Stalinist economic apparatus. Tito maintained the Marxist belief in the withering away of the state, and argued that in a socialist society state powers should be diminishing rather than building themselves up. In 1950 state ownership of industrial and commercial enterprises was abolished; the property of each enterprise was vested in its employees, and management taken over by 'workers' councils' elected by them. At the same time the Yugoslav economist Boris Kidric, who was president of the Economic Council and the Planning Commission, had come to the conclusion that central planning was inappropriate for the detailed decisions as to what consumer goods should be produced, and had concluded that a relatively free market should be set up for this purpose. Physical production targets were abolished, except for a very few basic commodities, and the workers' councils became free to decide how much to produce and at what prices to sell, i.e. to make the maximum profits. Although a large proportion of these profits go to the state, and another large proportion must be invested, the workers' councils have some freedom to decide how to dispose of the remainder, and they can also decide what form their investments shall take. Thus, although the state continues to decide what proportion of output is to be invested, the actual pattern of investment is largely unplanned and directed to where the highest returns are expected. More radical a departure still, Yugoslav agriculture was decollectivized in 1953, although an upper limit was set to holdings of land and machinery, and some co-operative enterprises remain.

The disturbances in Poland and the rising in Hungary in 1956 also led to some relaxation of Stalinism in those countries, as well as to the end of their exploitation by the USSR. The rate of growth of heavy industry was moderated, and a higher proportion of output diverted to satisfying consumers. In Poland agricultural collectivization was virtually abandoned, and in 1959 wholesale prices were reformed to give them the same relation to each other as on world markets, instead of their being arbitrarily fixed by the planners. This liberalization in satellite countries heralded similar changes in the Soviet Union itself. Stalin died in 1953, and three years later the Stalinist 'personality cult' was officially repudiated. The Khruschev régime admitted the backwardness of agriculture and announced that the time had now come when greater emphasis could be given to the production of consumer goods. Decollectivization was not considered to be the solution to Soviet agricultural problems; indeed before Stalin's death Khruschev had been responsible for the amalgamation of collective farms into still larger units. His main enthusiasm was for the opening up of more land in uncultivated areas, a programme which proved a failure. Agricultural taxes were reduced, however, and more investment promised. There was also a change in the planning process, which was decentralized. Instead of the main authority lying with a number of central industrial ministries, each dealing with their own products all over the USSR (and acting independently of each other), power was given to regional organizations dealing with everything produced in their areas. This was not so much an economic as a political move, increasing the powers of local party leaders at the expense of bureaucrats in the capital. The kind of planning carried out remained essentially the same, with the plans drawn up by local authorities submitted to the centre for co-ordination. The incredible ramifications of Soviet bureaucracy continued; P. J. D. Wiles quotes an example in 1960 of a motor factory which in order to procure ball-bearings from the factory next door had to despatch its indents with accompanying paper-work via 14 local and central government departments, within each of which the documents had to be circulated, checked and approved. The annual supply of ball-bearings from this one factory to the other involved papers weighing 100 lb. However, the trend to decentralization has been accompanied by a gradual increase in the powers of individual enterprises. A further major rationalization is now in process; by 1969 enterprises will not be considered to have fulfilled their targets unless they also manage to sell what they have produced.

While communist economic practice in the USSR and most Eastern European countries has seemed in recent years to be moving closer to Western ideas, the Chinese communist régime has been moving in the opposite direction. When the communists established control over the whole of mainland China in 1949, they enjoyed far more popular support than had been given to the Bolsheviks in 1918. China had suffered sporadic civil war for nearly 40 years, together with periodic foreign intervention. The peasants had been ruthlessly exploited by all the régimes they had known, and China was still an almost totally agricultural economy. The first years of communist rule restored order and stability.

Corruption and banditry disappeared; the land was distributed to the peasants. The terrible inflation of the last years of the civil war was dealt with by large-scale state trading for fixed prices; wages were fixed to prices and the rich were heavily taxed. Private enterprise in industry and trade was allowed to continue at first, alternately intimidated and denounced and provided with government loans, but the state acquired larger and larger shares in all firms until private ownership was gradually abolished.

It was soon apparent that the Chinese communists meant to develop the country along orthodox Stalinist lines, although it seemed at first that in agriculture at least they intended to avoid the Soviet mistakes. Their first Five Year Plan, announced in 1953, gave the usual enormous priority to investment in heavy industry. The emphasis was on developing an iron and steel industry, coal, electricity and heavy engineering, and Russian help was forthcoming for this; Soviet technicians designed and built plant and China paid in food and raw materials. It was claimed that the targets of the First Plan were exceeded by 17 per cent; in 1957 coal output was more than twice the largest output of any year before the communists took over, electricity generation had trebled, and steel output had grown from under a million tons to over five million.

Changes also began in agriculture in 1953. The peasants were now in possession of their holdings, taken over from the land-lords' estates. They were at first encouraged to form 'mutual aid' groups of about ten families, keeping their own land but pooling their labour and tools to co-operate at seed and harvest time. The next stage was for these groups to learn to co-operate all the year round, and in the original cautious approach to collectivization it was planned that only a third of all holdings would be organized in this way by 1957. But revolutionary pressures grew; the peasants were hurried into the third stage—the agricultural co-operative in which land was pooled but members were paid in relation to the amount of land they had contributed—and then into the fourth stage of full collectivization. The whole process was virtually complete by 1956. However, the smaller size of the collectives and the high calibre of many dedicated local officials still made the Chinese more successful than the Russians in the early stages of collectivization in the USSR. Grain output in 1957 was said to be 25 per cent greater than in any pre-communist year, and cotton output rose sharply.

At the end of the First Plan, the Chinese leaders made their fateful decision to make the 'great leap forward'. China was to become the world power her size and population warranted; the enormous disparities in wealth and industrialization between China and the present world powers was to be ended. Enthusiasm spread; local committees vied with each other in deciding to increase output to levels higher than the official goals. The final plans were absurd; steel production was to double in a year, and to this end rural resources were devoted to building 'backyard' blast furnaces whose products turned out to be virtually useless. In order to develop industry and agriculture together, the co-operatives were merged into communes, units of 20,000 or more members, spread over as many as a hundred villages. The communes constituted independent administrative and economic units, responsible for industry, agriculture, commerce, education and defence. The private plots which the peasants had so far been allowed to keep were abolished. Attempts were made to pay members in kind, though these were soon abandoned, but communal dining rooms and other facilities were encouraged as much as possible.

Just how disastrous the 'great leap forward' was for the Chinese economy is not known, since after 1959 no more production statistics were published. It was, however, apparent that there were food shortages; these would at first have been partly due to the droughts and floods of 1959, but in 1961–1964 China had to import large quantities of grain from the west. In 1960 came the quarrel with the de-Stalinizing USSR; Soviet experts were withdrawn and many projects had to be abandoned. It was announced that the main development effort would now be switched to agriculture; some of the communes broke up into co-operatives again, private plots were once more encouraged, and a free market was restored for the sale of their produce.

From recent developments in China, it would appear that these changes were successful in increasing standards of living. Mao Tse-tung's 'cultural revolution', which began early in 1967, appears to be partly directed against administrators who have followed the Soviet line of concentrating on increasing production, efficiency and wages rather than on the achievement of the classless society. This new crime has been labelled 'economism'; such officials are said to have ceased to be proletarian in outlook and to have become bourgeois. Mao's positive objectives are not yet clear. He appears to want a nation of communes, managed by the workers rather than the bureaucrats, but in practice this could only resemble the 'revisionist' Yugoslav system. It is hard to see how Mao's ideals can be realized except against a background of permanent chaos; in a state of revolution the primary concerns are political, but in a stable situation the hard-working Chinese are bound to increase production and standards of living rapidly, and to turn again to economic objectives.

CHAPTER SEVEN

The Developed Economies between the Wars

THE GREAT DEPRESSION OF THE 1930's

For a few years in the middle of the period between the two world wars, Marx's predictions of the course of economic history appeared about to be fulfilled. The capitalist economies of North America and Europe were unable to find markets for their products. Production and trade fell drastically, more and more millions became unemployed, and the declining prices of foodstuffs ruined farmers and reduced farm output while the population of industrial areas went hungry. The bankruptcy of laissez faire economics was apparent; there was no orthodox solution to the catastrophe. There seemed to be no means, within a society of free enterprise, of re-employing the labour force to produce even the goods and services which they themselves needed. Meanwhile in the USSR industrial production had begun to rise by a steady 10 per cent a year, in an economy largely insulated from the world depression by its independence of foreign trade and its strict government control over such imports and exports as there were. The Russians claimed that central planning and control in a socialist society would maintain this situation indefinitely; there could be no over-production in a society which distributed its output according to need, and no reason to slow down economic growth until all needs were satisfied. Mass unemployment was, as Marx had said, the inevitable consequence of capitalism, to which there would be no solution before the revolt of the working classes.

The First World War had left the Allied governments in varying states of economic health. At one extreme was Britain, whose industrial pattern had altered very little since the last century. The major British industries—textiles, coal, shipbuilding, iron and steel—all faced increased competition in overseas markets as a result of wartime expansion elsewhere, particularly by Japan and the USA. Their equipment also tended to be old-fashioned in comparison with that of their newer competitors. At the other extreme was the USA, whose production and exports had risen rapidly over the war years, and whose manufacturers were now well established in such new industries as motor vehicles, petroleum, tyres and various electrical consumer goods. Yet British economic policy was much the same as the American, except that Britain soon returned to free trade; it was believed that the sooner wartime controls could be abandoned and government expenditure cut back, the sooner production and trade would resume a steady upward trend. Like the other Allies, the British government was particularly anxious to return to the Gold Standard, then the symbol of a stable and ordered world.

World industrial production did show a steady increase for most of the 1920's, as did world trade, though with increased tariff barriers and the spread of industrialization, trade rose less rapidly than production. In Britain, however, manufacturing output did not catch up with its pre-war level until 1929; British exports did not recover their pre-war value till after the Second World War. The British economy needed re-shaping, but the initiative of private enterprise to enter new industries and rationalize and re-equip old ones was soon damped by the poor state of demand at home, and government leadership and support was not yet thought essential. There was a brief post-war enthusiasm for 'reconstruction'; the government was to lead a housing programme for 'homes for heroes', and discussed electrifying the railways, still under public control. But all such plans were quickly abandoned when the brief post-war boom broke. An Unemployment Act, passed in 1920, had brought nearly all employees into the national insurance scheme. It was assumed at the time that the maximum percentage of unemployed among members would be 4 per cent. By the summer of 1921 over 15 per cent of the labour force was unemployed; the lowest rate to be reached in the next twenty years was just under 10 per cent, and in the early 1930's the proportion was over 20 per cent.

In the USA, on the other hand, the laissez faire system was at the height of its success. In the 1920's the new American industries were booming. Motor vehicle production, which had been just over half a million in 1914, reached over 5 million by 1929. The petroleum and tyre industries grew at similar rates; huge investments were made in electricity generation, in electrical consumer goods and in housing. By the end of the decade, the US national income was larger than that of all the other main industrial countries added together, and with only 6 per cent of the world's population, the USA accounted for over 40 per cent of world manufacturing output. Foreign trade did not play much part in this expansion; by 1929 exports only accounted for 6 per cent of the American national income, and imports were still smaller than those of the UK. But if the outside world was relatively unimportant to the US, the USA was of crucial importance to the rest of the world. American imports of raw materials were the main expanding markets for many primary producers, and American investments abroad were now the main source of new capital. Consequently when the American economy collapsed in 1929, the world economy—apart from the USSR—fell with it.

The immediate cause of the Great Depression was that American consumption of the products of the main growth industries had temporarily reached saturation. Enough new housing had now been built for everyone who could afford it; the capacity of the motor industry to produce vehicles was now far ahead of sales, as was the case for motor tyres and most of the range of electrical goods. The sudden realization that this was the case, against a background of constantly rising share prices, led to the Wall Street crash in 1929, when shareholders panicked and sold out for anything they could get. The shock was tremendous; investment stopped almost overnight as capital owners refused to risk their remaining assets. Manufacturers started to cut back production and lay off their workers; domestic consumption fell as a result; production was cut still further and so on in a downwards spiral for three years. In 1932 there were 13 million American unemployed, gross national product had fallen by a third and industrial production by nearly half. American imports were less than a third of what they had been in 1929, and American net foreign lending had stopped.

Between the internationally interdependent Western economies unemployment is 'exportable'. All the countries trading with the USA in 1929 found their exports cut, the primary producers in particular. Unemployment and lower incomes followed in their export industries; since part of these incomes would normally have been spent on imports, imports then naturally fell in each of the countries concerned, in their turn affecting the export industries of all their trading partners. The decline in international trade was accelerated by a round of tariff increases; the Americans raised their tariffs in 1930 and all their trading partners rapidly retaliated, even Britain abandoning free trade in 1932. Trade was further restricted by the introduction of import quotas and exchange controls, and the laboriously reconstructed international monetary system began to break down again. Britain abandoned the Gold Standard in 1931, and three years later was followed by the USA and the other members of the gold bloc. World trade fell by 61 per cent between 1929 and 1932. Industrial production fell by 30 per cent in Britain and France and nearly 40 per cent in Germany. Unemployment spread throughout the non-communist world to reach an estimated 30 million in 1933.

THE WESTERN ALTERNATIVE TO LAISSEZ FAIRE

The revolution which eventually followed the Great Depression was not however a revolt of the working classes, but a complete change in the concept of the economic role of governments in democratic societies. The two men more responsible than any others for this change were the English economist J. M. Keynes and the American President Roosevelt. Keynes worked out the economic theory of how governments can control and stimulate economic growth, to avoid both the wastage of unemployment and the social disruption of inflation, without necessarily owning the means of production and exchange. Roosevelt hit upon Keynesian methods largely by following his own instincts.

Keynes (1883–1946) started on a civil service career, but soon returned to his university, Cambridge. He was a brilliant academic who was interested in economics as a means of determining government policy rather than as a pure science. In the First World War he joined the Treasury and was its Principal Representative at the Peace Conference; he resigned abruptly in 1919, giving his reasons in *The Economic Consequences of the Peace*. He returned to Cambridge, though he always maintained many non-academic interests; he was the chairman of an insurance company, the manager of an investment company, and was much concerned throughout his life with the arts in various forms. He served on several government committees as he returned to official favour, entered the Treasury again in the Second World War and was responsible for negotiating the American post-war loans to Britain and the Bretton Woods agreement which established the International Monetary Fund. His most important work, *The General Theory of Employment, Interest and Money*, was published in 1936.

Keynes argued that the level of employment in any one economy at any time depends on the expectations of employers about how much of anything they produce they can sell. This is the same as to say that employment depends on the level of what Keynes called 'aggregate demand' in the economy concerned. There are two main types of demand, for consumer goods and for investment goods, and if employment is to rise, either consumers' expenditure or investment expenditure, or both, must increase. When either of these falls, employment will also fall unless the other rises to balance it. In the depression of the 1930's, when investment expenditure in the USA suddenly stopped, manufacturers cut back production and reduced the numbers of their employees; consumption expenditure then also fell, since the unemployed spent less, and this in its turn created more unemployment and so on downwards.

According to Keynesian theory, therefore, a government which wants to change the level of employment in the economy can do so by influencing either the volume of consumers' expenditure or that of investment expenditure, or both. Consumers' expenditure does not simply depend on the number of people who are employed and earning steady incomes, but also what Keynes called 'the propensity to consume'. Any individual can decide not to spend some part of his income and to save it instead; the richer he is the greater scope he has to do this, while the very poor have little opportunity to save. This was one of the most revolutionary implications of Keynes' work; the ancient virtues of saving and abstinence could be shown, in certain economic circumstances, to be vices. Moreover, while saving by individuals might at times be undesirable, governments ought on occasion to be positively spendthrift. It had always been assumed that governments, like private households, should balance their budgets; Keynes showed that at times a government's first duty may be to increase the level of expenditure in the economy, and it may well be unable to do this except by deficit financing.

A government can increase consumers' expenditure, therefore, without taking direct action to see that more people are employed, by taxing people in the higher income brackets more heavily and redistributing the proceeds to people in the lower income brackets, in the confidence that they will spend nearly all the increase in their incomes. The redistribution can be achieved by reducing taxes for the lowest income groups, or by increasing social security benefits, and of course either of these steps may be taken without raising any other taxes if the government chooses to finance them from its existing revenues or by borrowing. There are also more subtle ways of persuading people to consume more or less, particularly in a rich country; a method commonly employed in the UK in recent years, where a high proportion of consumers' expenditure is made through hire purchase agreements, is to change the legal minimum initial deposit or the maximum repayment period allowed.

Keynes, however, tended to prefer the method of increasing investment as the more useful solution to the problem of unemployment. If a government wants to influence investment expenditure, it can do this directly by undertaking investment itself (or conversely by cutting back its existing projects). Keynes was responsible here for developing the very important concept of the 'multiplier'. He showed that if a government spends £1 million on, for example, a road building programme, a number of people are directly employed in building the road or making equipment with which to build it, and the income of all concerned rises by £1 million. But this is not all; the newly employed workers spend some of their extra income on consumer goods; this increases the numbers and raises the incomes of the consumer goods workers, who in turn spend their extra money on more consumer goods. The government therefore only needs to spend an initial £1 million to raise the income of the community by possibly several millions, and to give employment to far more people than can work on its own project. Governments can also influence investment expenditure by encouraging or discouraging private investment. This they can do by their control over the volume of money flowing into the economy, and of rates of interest. (In most Western economies the government can, through the Central Bank, control the rates of interest and other terms on which the commercial banks provide credit.) Company taxation can also be used for the same purpose, but this instrument takes longer to produce effects.

The discovery that a government can control the level of employment in the domestic economy through influencing consumption and investment had, as Keynes himself pointed out, major implications for international economic relations. Under the laissez faire system, a government faced with unemployment at home could only urge its producers to expand their exports, which would probably be at the expense of another country in a similar situation. Since by the early 1930's all countries had abandoned free trade, governments could also hope to provide more employment at home, again at the expense of their trading partners, by raising tariffs on imports. If nations could learn to achieve full employment by domestic policy, Keynes argued, 'there need be no important economic forces calculated to set the interest of one country against that of its neighbours. . . . International trade would cease to be what it is, namely, a desperate expedient to maintain employment at home by forcing sales on foreign markets and restricting purchases which, if successful, will merely shift the problem of unemployment to the neighbour which is worsted in the struggle, but a willing and unimpeded exchange of goods and services in conditions of mutual advantage.'[1]

[1] *General Theory of Employment, Interest and Money*, p. 382, Macmillan, 1954 ed.

In the conditions of the 1930's, however, international co-operation needed to come first. There could be only limited use in the application of Keynesian theory by individual governments while their trading partners continued to 'export' unemployment. Keynesian ideas were in fact hardly implemented between the wars, other than inadvertently. All governments reacted initially to the depression in the orthodox ways which were likely to make things worse, advocating cuts in wages in the hope of making exports cheaper and regardless of the effects on home consumption, and believing it to be their duty to cut their own expenditure and balance their budgets rather than to embark on expensive investment programmes. One of the British government's first reactions to depression was to abandon the idea of electrifying the railways, which would have just the sort of boost to the economy that Keynes would have recommended. Its extension of unemployment benefit for an indefinite period was the result more of humanitarian than economic policy, but this did serve to maintain consumption at a certain level, and it probably saved Britain from revolution. The British government never really accepted Keynesian ideas until the Second World War had started. The Popular Front government in France made some attempt to increase public spending in 1936, by which time the Fascist governments of Germany and Italy had begun to engage in public works with the idea of increasing employment together with national prestige. Only in the USA, after an early orthodox reaction to the collapse of the economy, was there a deliberate attempt to revive the economy by government action: President Roosevelt's National Recovery Act was passed three years before the *General Theory* was published. Price support, minimum wage legislation, social security benefits and public works, financed by budget deficits, helped the economy towards a slow revival, but unemployment remained high until the Second World War.

The trading policies of all the Western governments remained 'desperate expedients'. International co-operation to halt the decline in world trade proved impossible; the round of retaliatory tariff increases started off by the USA in 1930 expanded into the imposition of quotas and exchange controls. A World Economic

Conference was called in 1933 to try to reduce the rising barriers to trade, but it was a failure. The recovery of the Western economies was finally based on government spending, but it was spending on armaments; and the failure of international co-operation to solve the international economic crisis had enabled the Nazis to come to power in Germany.

The economic record of the Western governments in the period between the wars contrasted in many respects very unfavourably with that of the USSR. Total industrial production in the West in 1939 was little more than 10 per cent larger than in 1929. Industrial production in Russia had been rising by 10 per cent a year for most of this time and real national income per head by about 5 per cent a year. Theoretically, national income per head in Russia by 1939 had reached one-third of the British level, whereas it had been about one-sixth of the British level in 1913. The Western governments had been unable to prevent 30 million people from becoming unemployed; the Russians had no obvious unemployment problem. Yet by 1939 the foundations had been laid of an economic alternative to communism. The doctrines of laissez faire had finally been abandoned as unworkable, and the new theory of a government's responsibility for the control of economic affairs and of its capability of doing so had more or less been accepted. The workers of the Western countries had not revolted against capitalism; despite its inefficiencies, average standards of living had continued to improve over these twenty years, by a gradual redistribution of income when production did not increase. Real wages had risen for those in employment in Britain by 33 per cent between 1914 and 1939, and even for those who were unemployed conditions had improved: a working man living on unemployment benefit in 1934 was better off than an unskilled worker in employment in 1914. Moreover, the social services had everywhere continued to expand and benefits to become more generous, while the working week had grown shorter. Nor had the average Russian worker received an annual increase of 5 per cent in his income during the 1930's; an enormous proportion of the Soviet national income was being re-invested. The relentless pursuit of agricultural collectivization —sometimes estimated to have led to a million deaths—meant that food supplies were never enough, and the production of all consumer goods was held back to allow heavy industry to achieve its rapid growth. The mass arrests and deaths from starvation under Stalinism have to be set against the miseries of mass unemployment under capitalism.

CHAPTER EIGHT

The Underdeveloped Countries' Colonial Background

THE ECONOMICS OF COLONIALISM

Most underdeveloped countries are ex-colonies, or were for a time under the 'protection' of a developed country. It is sometimes argued, particularly in the ex-colonies proper, that generations of exploitation by the colonizing powers must account, at least in part, for their present poverty. In this view colonialism was a purely economic phenomenon, a view which is reinforced by Marxist teaching, according to which colonialism is the last desperate attempt by a declining capitalist society to find new markets for its over-produced commodities. It is certainly true that economic motives have been dominant in the policies of most colonizing powers, but the reasons for colonial annexation have also been political, strategic, and at least for many of the individuals concerned, ethical. Hence few explanations of colonial history that are made purely in terms of economics quite make sense.

It has sometimes been argued on the other side that the 'balance sheet of imperialism' adds up the other way; that trade in the raw materials of the overseas territories and the manufactures of Europe would have developed to a profitable extent without the annexation of colonies, while the expense of their administration and the flow of capital abroad was largely to Europe's disadvantage, in particular to that of the UK, which since the end of the nineteenth century has always been behind in investment in its own economy. This is a calculation which it is impossible to pursue, although instances can certainly be found of occasions on which the actual profits of colonialism to the colonizer were plainly non-existent. It is equally impossible to say of any individual underdeveloped country—except perhaps of the countries of South-East Asia ravaged by lengthy wars for independence—that it would now be in a more prosperous state if it had never been a colony. Colonialism in modern times has always brought with it a certain amount of economic development, even if the profits from this have been entirely repatriated and the development itself has not been of the sort which would have been most beneficial to the country concerned. The large amounts of capital which flowed from the last quarter of the nineteenth century onwards from Europe overseas went either to European colonies or to countries settled by European populations where investment also seemed relatively secure. It seems most unlikely that any substantial European investment would have been received by Asia or Africa under other circumstances. Trade, in so far as it did not depend on expensive development, is of course another matter.

NINETEENTH-CENTURY COLONIAL EXPANSION

Early European colonial annexation was certainly for almost entirely economic, and hence in a sense exploitative, motives—to secure monopolies of trade with newly-discovered or newly-accessible territories, and also to settle surplus population. When, early in the nineteenth century, it began to be argued that colonies were in fact of no economic value, colonialism went out of fashion. Two major areas of colonial territories, South America and the USA, had now broken free of European control, and the new school of economists explained that according to free trade theory a monopoly of trade with another country could only be generally disadvantageous. They could quote the expansion of trade between Britain and the USA since the latter's independence to prove their point, and indeed for rapidly industrializing Britain there was no need for protected overseas markets. This being the case, there were few reasons left for maintaining colonies. One of these was the possibility of European emigration, which seemed to philanthropically-minded economists to be the only hope of breaking out of the vicious circle of the 'iron law' of wages. The other was the new, vaguely-formulated concept of the responsibility of the 'higher' civilizations towards the rest. James Mill, who argued that colonies were always likely to be an expense rather than a source of wealth to their possessor, nevertheless observed of India in 1810 that 'whatever may be our sense of the difficulties into which we have brought ourselves by the improvident assumption of such a dominion, we earnestly hope, for the sake of the natives, that it will not be found necessary to leave them to their own direction'.[1]

No great power was, however, likely to undertake further colonial expansion 'for the sake of the natives' alone. For the greater part of the nineteenth century, there were very few colonial developments. As far as Britain was concerned, new colonies were established in Australia and New Zealand to settle British emigrants, and the future total independence of the 'white' colonies within the Commonwealth was foreshadowed when the Durham Commission, set up after a rebellion in Canada in 1837, outlined the idea of an association of self-governing countries. The developing concept of responsibility for indigenous colonial peoples was involved in the British government's decision to take over the administration of India in 1858 from the British East India Company. Otherwise there were few extensions of British control until the 1880's. The other powers showed a similar lack of interest in colonies, although France acquired Algiers in 1830 and parts of Indo-China and Somaliland in 1862. Bismarck even refused to buy Mozambique from Portugal when it was offered to Germany.

In the last quarter of the century, however, there was a complete reversal in attitudes to colonialism. This was directly related to a change in international economic relationships. Other countries besides Britain had undergone industrial revolutions, and Britain's supremacy in export markets was being challenged. All the industrialized countries wanted to sell their manufactures abroad, and this led to a new interest in colonialism with, as far as the continental powers were concerned, the prospect of establishing trade monopolies. For Britain, free trade remained a basic principle of economic policy, but the possibility of the exclusion

[1] *Edinburgh Review*, April 1810: quoted in Donald Winch, *Classical Political Economy and Colonies*, L.S.E., 1965.

of British goods from wide areas of the world naturally pointed to the necessity of colonial expansion by Britain as well. Besides the new competition for export markets, the pattern of imports was changing. New commodities, or enormously increased quantities of old ones, were needed by modern industries; more prosperous populations in Europe and North America demanded more varied food. The availability of imports for industry such as rubber, oilseeds, jute and tin, or of tea, coffee, cocoa and tropical fruits for consumers, depended on investment in plantations, mines and other enterprises in their countries of origin. There were obvious deterrents to private enterprise in making such investments unless it was certain that the territory concerned would not be annexed by another foreign power, usually a more serious prospect than the problems presented by local populations, and commercial interests consequently brought increasing pressure to bear on their governments to assert their national claims.

Such major economic reasons underlie the enormous colonial expansion which took place at this time. Indo-China, Burma, Malaya, New Guinea, the Fiji Islands, and almost the whole of the continent of Africa were annexed by the various European powers. The US acquired the Philippines and Hawaii; Japan took large tracts of Chinese territory, and while the rest remained nominally independent, a considerable part was divided into European spheres of influence in which the Chinese were forced to grant trading concessions.

Even at this time, however, there were many non-economic reasons, in several individual cases, for the establishment of colonial rule. National prestige was a major factor, particularly for France after the humiliation of the Franco-Prussian war, and as the new colonialism developed it became a sufficient reason for annexation even where there was no evident economic advantage to be gained. Russia's considerable expansion of her eastern and southern frontiers, which also took place at this time, was largely of this nature. The British government, under the influence of Lord Salisbury, resisted commercial and patriotic pressure groups for some time, but eventually joined in the scramble with the rest—British territory expanded by nearly 4 million square miles between 1884 and 1900, French territory by 3·5 million square miles and Germany's by over 1 million. British expansion was nevertheless left in the first instance mainly to private enterprise, the normal pattern in Africa and South-East Asia at this time being through the granting of a charter to a private company to occupy a certain stretch of territory in order to secure the pre-eminence of British trade. The companies' shareholders provided the finance and their employees the administration of the territory. Very few ever showed a profit, but once British rule had been introduced through a company it was always felt politically unacceptable to withdraw, and most of the companies were bought out by the government. Direct rule would follow, establishing the colonies proper that the French and German governments acquired at once.

The other factor in the colonial expansion of this era was philanthropic and applied mainly to British annexation in East and Central Africa. The African continent had been subjected to the worst possible form of exploitation by foreigners, the slave trade. It has been estimated that 7 million West Africans were landed in the Americas in the eighteenth century and some 4 million in the nineteenth. Livingstone and other explorers estimated the annual loss of population to Central and East Africa as a result of the Arab slave trade during the second half of the nineteenth century at perhaps half a million a year, although of this a comparatively small number actually survived the slave raids and walked to the coast to be exported. Populations were decimated and whole areas laid waste. The development, early in the nineteenth century, of the European conscience about the slave trade, and the organization of pressure on governments first to ban it for their own nationals and then to engage in international action to bring it to an end, is an early parallel to the more recent development of a conscience in the developed countries about the problems of the underdeveloped; it was the first example of an active international concern for sufferings abroad. It was a part of an evangelical movement which sent both Protestant and Roman Catholic missionaries to Africa throughout the century, who were responsible for much of its exploration. The missionaries saw that the establishment of legitimate commerce would be a major weapon against the slave trade, and consequently normally welcomed the appearance of the chartered companies; the British Imperial East Africa Company, which made an enormous loss, was indeed established with funds partly subscribed by mission supporters. The missionaries did not in the first place expect or wish for colonial annexation, but the advent of traders inevitably provoked the interest of foreign powers and conflict with Arab and other hostile forces, so that the missions' supporters at home also began to campaign for the declaration of at least British 'spheres of influence' in their areas.[1]

After the phase of colonial expansion based on this strange mixture of philanthropy and international jealousy, the final phase of European annexation, stretching into the twentieth century, was dominated by strategic motives. Strategy remained an acceptable argument for colonialism far longer than economics or philanthropy, although as a basis for colonial rule it must be the least likely to involve advantages for the colonial people concerned. The control of the Suez Canal, the short route to India (and also security for Britain's share of Egypt's debts), was the reason for the British annexation of Egypt in 1882. The need to secure supplies of Middle East oil in time of war led to the establishment of British and French control over much of the Middle East during and after the First World War, although outright colonial annexation did not follow. Britain acquired Cyprus at the same time as a base for control of the Eastern Mediterranean.

TWENTIETH-CENTURY COLONIALISM

The notion of European superiority suffered a severe blow in the First World War. When Germany's colonies were divided

[1] It is interesting to compare the histories of the annexation of Rhodesia and Uganda. The one was a mixture of economic motives— valuable minerals were anticipated—and international jealousies, and the other a mixture of international jealousies and philanthropy, there being no question of profit in the foreseeable future. They are well described respectively in *The Birth of a Dilemma* (*the conquest and settlement of Rhodesia*), Philip Mason, OUP, 1958, and in the first volume of Margery Perham's *Lugard*, Collins, 1956.

between the Allies afterwards they were accepted from the League of Nations in a new spirit, at least on paper, to be governed as 'a sacred trust of civilization' until such time as they were able to 'stand on their own feet in the arduous conditions of the modern world'. The notion that colonial powers had an active responsibility for colonial development was, however, born at a time when colonies had once more begun to seem of little economic value. With the war over, primary products were reaching a state of over-production which was to become increasingly serious. Most of tropical Africa, once no other power was competing for it, appeared to be little but a liability to its owners. India also seemed to be losing its value to Britain; once the market for a quarter of Britain's textile exports, she had now started to manufacture her own and was importing from Japan. Indonesia and Malaya faced declining markets for rubber, their main support. Depression among the primary producers was soon to be followed by the world depression, when governments believed that their only remedy was to cut public expenditure. While the colonial powers were prepared to encourage colonial development, therefore, their main object was that the colony should not be an expense to the European taxpayer, and the idea that financial assistance should be provided from Europe was slow to be accepted. Investment was left almost wholly to private enterprise, except for occasional grants for railway or port development.

The change in attitudes was nevertheless apparent in the colonial governments' assumption of responsibility for social as well as basic economic development, even if these continued to be financed from scanty surplus local revenues. The difference now became apparent between British colonial policy on the one hand and that of the French, Portuguese and other European colonizers on the other; the British, while not anticipating colonial independence, except perhaps for India, in the foreseeable future, nevertheless expected their colonies to develop in some sense along their own lines, while the other Europeans in theory saw the subjects of their empires as eventually wholly adopting their own cultures. This had radical implications for colonial education policies, the British tending to give priority to the widest possible spread of a limited form of education, the 'assimilationists' con-centrating on the education of an *élite*, who often had the oppor-tunity of completing their studies in the mother country and who would become in effect Frenchmen or Portuguese. It also had important implications for the development of colonial societies, the British attitude fostering and itself partly deriving from racial prejudice and encouraging colour bars. Yet the British concept of colonialism admitted the prospect of independence more easily, although this included independence for colonies controlled by white settler minorities. The theory of assimilation did not admit the possibility of independence—'L'Algerie, c'est la France'— but enabled the mother countries to maintain a much firmer grip on their own settlers.

Another consequence of the depression was a revival of interest in colonies as markets. The French, Belgians and Dutch took further steps to turn their dependencies into closed trading areas; the Japanese carried this policy to even greater lengths in the territories they had taken from China. The idea of 'imperial preference', mooted since the end of the last century, became increasingly popular in Britain; it was argued that Britain should abandon free trade except with the Empire, from which food and raw materials should continue to enter duty free, while the dominions and colonies would give preference to British manu-factures. This plan was of course aimed at the developed markets of Canada, Australia, New Zealand and South Africa, and to some extent India, rather than the much poorer colonies. Not surprisingly the dominions, virtually independent sovereign states since 1918, steadily resisted making any concessions to Britain which would further discourage their own industries. The only result of the long campaign for Empire Free Trade was that when Britain herself finally abandoned free trade in 1932 she exempted imports from the dominions and colonies from the new duties. The dominions gave some preference to British goods, not by cutting their tariffs but by raising them still further on imports from other sources; the colonies gave no preferences, but govern-ment purchasing policies and the predominance of British-owned enterprises usually ensured that they would buy British where possible in any case. These arrangements had an appreciable effect on the pattern of trade; the proportion of British imports deriving from the dominions, India and the colonies rose from 24 per cent in 1931 to 37 per cent in 1937, while the proportion of exports going to the Empire rose from 32 per cent to 39 per cent.

A major event in colonial economic history occurred in 1929, when (in a hope of developing new markets for British exports) the British government took powers to lend or give money to colonies to help stimulate further investment. The Colonial Development Fund was established for this purpose. The sums in question were still very small—only £4 million went to the whole of British Africa between 1929 and 1938—and development remained slow, but the basic principle of aid from Europe was established. Colonial development was in fact infinitely more stimulated by the Second World War, with the accompanying rapid increase in demand for food and raw materials, accelerated for the other primary producers when the Japanese cut off supplies from the colonies of South-East Asia. Colonies suddenly became once again economically valuable. The mining industries of the Congo and Rhodesia boomed, as did West African oilseeds and cocoa; several African countries built up large reserves during the war years from the high prices paid for their products at a time when there were few imports available on which the proceeds could be spent. After the war ended, therefore, development could proceed much more rapidly, assisted by greatly increased aid from Britain and France to their colonies, and by several years in which world prices for primary commodities continued to rise.

The rapidity with which colonial empires were dismantled after 1945 was in strange contrast to the very slow progress towards independence which was made in the years between the wars. India had been promised 'responsible government' as early as 1917; Gandhi launched his first civil disobedience campaign in 1920, and various steps towards self-government were made until a firm promise of independence after the war was given in 1942. Similar steps had been taken in Ceylon and Burma, and the US promised ultimate independence to the Philippines during the 1930's. Elsewhere there seemed in 1939 no foreseeable prospect of independence, and least of all in Africa. But the ideas of colonial peoples and to some extent those of their governors were totally altered by the war. The Japanese occupation of the British, Dutch and French colonies of South-East Asia demonstrated that Europeans were no longer invincible. The examples of India and the Philippines showed that colonial powers might be prepared to surrender their possessions peaceably. The USA and the USSR, both, in theory, opposed to colonialism,[1] had become the dominant world powers, and could give official support to colonial freedom movements through the United Nations. The colonies which had been League of Nations mandates were now reconstituted as UN trust territories, with the agreement of all the powers responsible for administering them, except South Africa, and with the new obligation to prepare them for independence. As far as Britain was concerned, crippled by the expense of the war, and with a Labour government with new ideals in power, colonial independence as soon as practicable was accepted policy. It was followed with few deviations except where 'strategic' arguments were put forward or where white settler populations fought a delaying action. The French concept of empire was harder to adapt, and long wars for independence were fought in Algeria and Indo-China. The Dutch fought for a short time to keep Indonesia, which had considerable economic value to them; the Belgians for the same reason resisted the idea of independence for the Congo until they were threatened by the prospect of fighting to keep it, and the Portuguese still cling anachronistically to their African colonies.

THE COLONIAL BALANCE SHEET

While it is impossible as yet—and probably always will be—to draw up anything like a complete balance sheet of colonialism,

[1] Although the USSR was in fact practising an extreme form of political and economic colonialism in Eastern Europe at the time. The US also tends to be accused of 'neo-colonialism' almost as often as the ex-colonial powers proper, in view of the heavy dependence of many South American countries on US trade and capital.

there are certain obvious economic and social consequences of their colonial past which affect independent underdeveloped countries today. These appear both on the credit and the debit side of the account, although at the present time, as newly independent countries realize how poor they are and how limited their immediate prospects of improvement, the debits of colonialism are their main preoccupation.

There is little difference, from the point of view of the ex-colonies, between the past activities in their countries of private foreign traders and investors and those of foreign governments. In fact in assessing the colonial record it should be remembered that private trade, at least, would have developed on similar lines even if European governments had never intervened; most of Africa and Asia were indeed opened up to the outside world by private traders in the first place. The most obvious form of exploitation for which colonial régimes are blamed, the exchange of manufactures useless for economic development, such as beads, alcohol, firearms and cloth, for the most valuable colonial commodities, was the inevitable result of the first impact of industrialized Europe upon the underdeveloped world; private enterprise was bound to satisfy evident local demands. This is not to say that as time went on many colonial régimes could not have done more to curb exploitation by traders, who frequently supplied shoddy manufactures at high prices and obtained primary commodities in exchange for much less than they were worth.[1]

The colonial régimes themselves, once established, all made some contribution to economic development. With great variations from colony to colony, they established the beginnings of an economic infrastructure, building railways and roads, developing water and electricity supplies, and embarking on education and medical services. Research into tropical diseases was one of colonialism's major contributions to the underdeveloped world. In conjunction with private enterprise, the colonial governments introduced new crops and new methods of growing them, and opened up other forms of primary production—forestry, fisheries

[1] Some examples are quoted in *False Start in Africa*, René Dumont, André Deutsch, 1966.

and in particular mining. The West Indian sugar industry is one of the earliest examples of a purely colonial economic development; plantation agriculture and modern mining industries throughout Asia and Africa were later organized from Europe. Many of what are today Africa's main food and cash crops are not native to the continent, but were introduced from South America, while others grew wild but were not cultivated before the Europeans arrived. The early Portuguese colonizers introduced cassava, maize and sweet potato; the late nineteenth-century arrivals brought cocoa and sisal and began the cultivation of coffee and cotton. The price paid by colonial peoples for such developments was in the alienation of their land—never in fact on a very large scale but bitterly resented where it occurred—and in the process of learning to conform to the demands of a wage economy. This included some of the blackest marks against colonialism, such as the appalling record of forced labour in the rubber plantations of the Belgian Congo; and yet the eventual development of a labour force used to fixed wages and hours of work was a useful economic inheritance for many now independent countries.

Perhaps the claim most often put forward by the colonialists themselves in favour of their occupation has been that they imposed peace and efficient central government on territories otherwise subject to recurrent violence and ruled by numerous and often tyrannical authorities. This claim usually has considerable substance, and peace and efficient administration are major contributions to economic development. But this achievement often had other and less useful aspects. The African territories endowed with the advantage of firm central rule were divided up in Europe, according to a pattern which any study of a map of Africa will show to have little relation to economic or ethnic considerations. These arbitrary frontiers have been one of the main factors in the political disturbances which have so often followed independence. Moreover the elimination of local forms of government—although certain colonial régimes made considerable if inevitably distorted attempts to maintain them—left post-colonial Africa with an inheritance of an alien form of administration which, while effective, is extremely expensive and operated by civil servants whose standards of living are far above those of the rest of their people. This burden of expense has been notably increased for the most 'balkanized' parts of Africa by the desire of many newly independent countries to maintain as wide a diplomatic representation abroad as possible. It is not of course essential for independent countries to continue to pay their own nationals on the same scale that the European administrators received, but very few countries have made significant changes in this respect. One colonial inheritance for African countries is consequently extremely inequitable income distribution, which it is hard to imagine could have developed to this extent in so short a time otherwise, and administration by officials who seem to inhabit another world from that of the peasant farmers who pay most of the taxes. Elsewhere, however, great disparities in standards of living existed before the colonialists arrived, and European administration in Asia can often take credit for an opposite effect.

The actual level and value of colonial and social development varied considerably from colony to colony. This was mainly in relation to the natural resources available, although not in the case of one of the most crucial factors for future development, the extent to which the colonial people had been trained to take over their own administration. This varied from the situation in India, where the civil service had been integrated at all levels for some years and the supply of graduates and other professional people was beginning to be comparable to that of the poorer European countries, to the state of affairs in the Belgian Congo, where the administration had actually forbidden Congolese to receive any higher education, at home or abroad, until 1955, five years before independence. The method of withdrawal by the colonial régime also varied, with considerable implications for the maintenance of development. There were departures planned over a number of years of shared government, ending with a capital grant from Europe and with a substantial number of colonial officials remaining to continue their work until they could be replaced (broadly the situation for most of British Africa), and there were abrupt decisions to leave such as that taken by the French when Guinea voted in 1958 for complete independence rather than to remain within the French Community; all French officials were immediately withdrawn, taking all the government files with them, and all aid was stopped.

The most basic criticism of colonialism does not however lie in its individual social and economic failures, which can always be countered by outstanding examples of development. It consists rather of its inevitable tendency to distort the development of the economy concerned into directions primarily favourable to the ruling country. This meant that although development took place in most colonies, it was not necessarily of a kind which made the best possible use (for the colony concerned) of the resources employed, nor which made all possible use of local resources. One of the best, if extreme, examples of this kind of economic distortion was a scheme carried out by a government exceptionally enlightened as to its responsibilities for the development of colonies towards independence—the Groundnuts Scheme for Tanganyika initiated by the British Labour government of 1946. The primary object of this scheme was to supplement Britain's post-war shortage of oils and fats, and the government was enthusiastic over a plan that would simultaneously promote the development of Tanganyika. It was intended that the project would eventually be handed over by the government corporation initially running it to African farmers. But there could have been no question of spending the £24 million the scheme was expected to cost on a single project of colonial aid as such. The total spent was in fact £35 million, of which when the scheme was wound up £25 million was officially admitted to have been lost—the areas chosen did not have ground or rainfall suitable for growing groundnuts. Some of the remaining £10 million did benefit Tanganyika; it was spent on a new port, on training a number of Tanganyikans in various skills, and on housing, cleared land and other developments in the groundnut areas, two of which are now successfully used for cattle ranching and tobacco growing. Had the original main objective been the development of these areas for African farming, however, it is inconceivable that pre-liminary research would not have been made into what could actually be grown there; Tanganyikan development would have been boosted by nearly four times the amount of capital expenditure, and there would have been additional benefits to the countries trading with her.

The spurt forward taken by many colonial economies in the years immediately following independence—although these were usually years of falling prices for primary producers—is evidence of the value of truly independent economic policies. The distorting effect of colonialism is clearest in the pattern of the colonies' trade before independence; Nigeria for instance sent 50 per cent of exports to and received 40 per cent of imports from the UK, and the proportions for Algeria in relation to France were 80 per cent and 90 per cent. Many ex-colonies, once able to make their own agreements with foreign traders and investors of all nationalities, have been able to expand their exports (although in recent trade conditions this has often only meant maintaining their value), by diversifying their markets. Most are nevertheless still heavily dependent on the countries which once ruled them to buy their products, and as the underdeveloped countries have watched the prices of their exports fall in the years since most of them gained their independence, this has become one of the most bitterly resented inheritances of colonialism.

CHAPTER NINE

The Three Groups of Economies since 1945

THE POST-WAR SITUATION

The economic situation of the West at the end of the Second World War was in many ways very similar to that of 1918, except that Europe had this time suffered far greater destruction and damage. There were enormous losses in housing and in industrial plant; industrial production in Western Europe as a whole in 1946 was less than three-quarters of what it had been before the war, while in the western zone of Germany it was under a third. As in the First World War, international trade had been distorted from its normal patterns, Europe and Asia having been largely cut off from the rest of the world for the war years. Once again, inflation was severe and prices were rising rapidly, though at widely varying rates, in different countries. Throughout Europe there was a huge pent-up demand for imports of all kinds—food, raw materials consumer goods, and machinery and equipment with which to start industry going again—but accompanied by a severe shortage of foreign exchange with which to pay for them. The American economy had as before grown rapidly in the war years, and the US was now the main source for most of the imports that Europe needed for reconstruction; the shortage of dollars to pay for these was a major economic preoccupation. The European governments were obliged to maintain severe restrictions on all international trade; each country had to balance its trade with each of its trading partners individually to avoid exchange problems, and international trade was increasingly carried out by means of elaborate inter-governmental 'bilateral' agreements for specified goods in specified quantities.

As in 1918, the USSR had suffered more from the war than any other country. It was however now firmly established as the second world power, and was able at the end of the war and during the next three years to line its western borders with satellite communist countries. Some of these were obliged to provide the Soviet Union with valuable raw materials and manufactures as a form of war reparations. The strength of the communist bloc was also about to be increased by the accession of China. Of the three groups of economies, however, it was the primary producers whose position was most radically different from that of 1918. The high war-time demand for food and raw materials was on this occasion sustained for a decade afterwards. The high prices paid for them by European buyers were of greater direct benefit to the underdeveloped economies concerned than before the war, particularly in British Africa where government purchasing agreements had tended to reduce the profits of the private trader. Since there was at the same time a shortage of imports from Europe, many of these countries built up substantial reserves with which development could now be initiated. Indian independence was declared, and independence movements everywhere began to gather momentum.

Although the facts of international economic life did not differ substantially, except for primary producers, in 1945 from 1918, the economic policies and beliefs of Western governments at least had undergone a transformation. As far as domestic policies were concerned, governments had accepted that they could and should control the level of economic activity, although the degree of official commitment to such policies varied considerably. Internationally, they had accepted that co-operation was essential to restore and maintain prosperity. This radical change in international attitudes had begun during the war, with the American provision of aid to the other Allied governments with no obligations to repay it.[1] It was summarized in the United Nations Charter, with all its hopes for political, social and economic co-operation, and the pattern of international economic co-operation in particular was planned in 1944 when the representatives of 44 nations met at Bretton Woods (New Hampshire), and signed the Articles of Agreement for the International Monetary Fund and the International Bank for Reconstruction and Development.

[1] 'Lend-Lease'; the only obligation to repay was in kind, in the improbable event of the Allies having anything the US wanted.

The object of the signatories to the Bretton Woods agreement was to create institutional arrangements to prevent the international breakdown of the 1930's from ever recurring. The first requirement was a smoothly functioning international monetary system, which would provide the stability of the old gold standard without its inflexibility. Such a system had to provide sufficient international 'liquidity' (in the form of reserves and credit facilities) to finance world trade; it had to encourage stable exchange rates and orderly exchange arrangements while making it possible for exchange rates to be altered when necessary without a round of competitive changes following, and it had to provide other adjustment mechanisms which would allow balance of payments problems to be financed without the country concerned needing to resort to domestic policies involving rapidly rising prices or unemployment, or to international policies involving restrictions on trade or capital movements. There was no general agreement on the best way of establishing such a system; the two main plans, the British plan drawn up by Keynes and the American plan drawn up by Harry D. White,[1] were finally blended in the creation of the IMF.[2] Under its original provisions a stock of international credit facilities was built up by means of each member contributing a quota, a quarter in gold and the rest in the member's own currency. From this stock it was agreed that each member should be allowed to borrow when in need up to twice its own quota. Proposed changes in exchange rates were to be submitted to the Fund for international agreement, but in view of the experience of the 1930's, members were allowed to impose independent restrictions on short-term capital movements in and out of their countries, and also to discriminate against trade partners whose currencies had become scarce in the Fund.

The second institution established as a result of Bretton Woods, the International Bank for Reconstruction and Development, which is commonly known as the World Bank, was designed to provide capital for countries needing it to repair war damage or for economic development. Between the wars, independent underdeveloped countries wanting to borrow money abroad had only

[1] Director of Monetary Research in the US Treasury Department.
[2] The IMF will be more fully discussed in Chapter 14.

been able to do so at very high interest rates; the fall in commodity prices had often made their payment impossible. It was intended that the IBRD should provide loans on reasonable terms, from funds built up partly from the subscriptions of member governments and partly from private money borrowed by the Bank.

It was intended to establish a third international institution to control the reformed world economy, the International Trade Organization, but although this was agreed by a conference at Havana, the agreement was not ratified by the US Senate. The objects of the ITO were, however, largely included in the General Agreement on Tariffs and Trade (GATT), which was signed in 1947. GATT laid down fixed rules for international trading relations, with the basic principles that governments should consult each other before increasing trade restrictions, and that members should work towards the reduction of barriers to international trade. Meanwhile trade restrictions should be confined to tariffs, which leave a way open to really competitive trading partners, rather than include quotas which ban further trade altogether, and members should not discriminate between one another, but should aim to treat all trading partners equally on the basis of the treatment given to the 'most favoured nation'. This last provision had been a major objective for the US. Although members agreed to work towards eliminating existing preferences, and to grant no new ones, the establishment of free trade areas or customs unions[1] were declared to be exceptions to the rule.

The initial signatories to these three international agreements were in general all the Western developed countries, and the main independent or effectively independent countries of South America, Asia and Africa. The USSR refused invitations to participate, and Eastern European countries like Poland and Czechoslovakia which joined at first were later obliged to withdraw, though Czechoslovakia remained a member of GATT.

---

[1] In a free trade area, goods flow freely between members without obstacles in the form of tariffs or quantitative restrictions, but members continue to decide their individual trade policies with countries outside it. In a customs union, there are no internal restrictions on trade, and members also agree on a common tariff wall against the outside world.

THE UNIFICATION OF EUROPE

The economics and politics of the post-war world were, however, to develop in ways which had not been predicted at the end of the war. The international institutions which were created to prevent the repetition of the experiences of the 1930's proved in many ways inadequate for the problems of the second half of the century, and the degree of international control and co-operation which developed was in some ways less than had been hoped. The non-participation of the USSR was not a surprise, but the greatly increased size of the communist bloc and its apparently permanent division of Europe had not been fully envisaged. The emergence of continental Western Europe as an economic entity separate from the UK, with trade and financial policies tending to differ from those of the UK and the USA, was a new divisive factor. Finally there was the rapid movement to independence of Europe's colonies, and the subsequent appearance of an enormous group of independent underdeveloped countries with urgent requirements for foreign capital and export markets, and no longer bound to rely for these on Western economies.

The inadequacy of the IMF to deal with the post-war monetary situation became apparent at once. The initial Fund was not nearly large enough to supply Europe's dollar needs; the economic outlook in Europe grew rapidly worse, despite American loans. The situation was saved by the unprecedentedly generous international action of the US, with the proposal in 1947 of Marshall Aid. The speech in which Secretary of State Marshall announced America's intentions is a classic statement of international economic interdependence: 'Aside from the demoralizing effect on the world at large and the possibilities of disturbances arising as a result of the desperation of the people concerned, the consequences to the economy of the United States should be apparent to all. It is logical that the United States should do whatever it is able to do to assist in the return of normal economic health in the world, without which there can be no political stability and no assured peace. Our policy is directed not against any country or doctrine but against hunger, poverty, desperation and chaos.'

The US offered to provide financial assistance on whatever scale was necessary to solve Europe's recovery problems. The Americans did not believe that this could be achieved by individual countries acting independently; they considered indeed that Europe's future must lie in a United States of Europe, and meanwhile offered Marshall Aid to all European nations, including the Eastern countries, who were prepared to plan and co-operate in a joint programme of recovery. The USSR's refusal of aid on these terms for herself and her satellites was one of the main events in the post-war division of the world into the Western and Eastern blocs. Western Europe accepted the offer. The Committee of European Co-operation was formed by all countries except Finland and Spain to draw up the initial programme; it was soon replaced by a permanent Organization for European Economic Co-operation (OEEC).[1] OEEC members undertook to draw up national targets for 1952, when American aid was intended to end, to consider the possibilities of collective planning in such fields as electricity and steel, and to abolish trade restrictions between each other as rapidly as possible. The OEEC administration co-ordinated the various national plans, and arranged the distribution of aid between countries. US aid to Europe was at this time running initially at about 2·5 per cent of US national income; it amounted finally to nearly $30 billion, of which over two-thirds was in the form of straight grants. The IMF's total initial resources, in contrast, were $7 billion. An organization within OEEC, the European Payments Union, arranged payments between European countries and provided automatic credits—unlike the formal borrowing arrangements set up for the IMF—for countries in deficit with their fellow EPU members.

The Marshall Aid programme was the beginning of several modern economic relationships. As was intended, it enabled the economies of Western Europe to regain their pre-war prosperity in a very short time. Its other effects were to accentuate the division between East and West, and to provide the basis for the

[1] OEEC became OECD—the Organization for Economic Co-operation and Development—in 1961, when its membership was extended to non-European countries (the US, Canada and Japan) and it became an international organization for economic planning and research.

unification of continental Western Europe. The Americans had been anxious to encourage the unification of Europe as a whole; their aid had been conditional upon European co-operation, and they had assisted OEEC to set up machinery for the liberalization of European trade and payments while accepting discrimination against their own exports. They had believed that only a united Europe would be a sufficiently viable economic and political unit to stand up to encroachment from the East. Their expectations as to the political constitution of such an economic entity were somewhat vague, but within Europe the dream of a federation of countries ruled by a supra-national organization had existed for centuries. The movement for a united Europe found its opportunity in the basic degree of co-operation established for the distribution of Marshall Aid. In 1948 a customs union was finally consolidated between Belgium, the Netherlands and Luxembourg (Benelux), the first landmark in the general progress towards unification. In 1950 the French government, seeing that control over the Ruhr was likely to be restored to the Germans in the near future, and determined to avoid the unrestricted revival of German power, gave its backing to the Schuman[1] Plan. Schuman's proposal was to solve this long-established political problem and at the same time make an important contribution to European economic development by amalgamating the coal and steel industries of France, West Germany, the Benelux countries and Italy under the control of a supra-national High Authority, in which all members would participate equally.

The agreement to set up the European Coal and Steel Community revealed the first major break between Britain and Europe. Britain could not accept the surrender of national policy to a supra-national authority, in particular at that time in view of its own Labour government and the very remote prospect of a socialist majority in the other six countries. This consideration no longer applied for Britain after 1951, when the Six moved on to propose the establishment of a complete customs union, but Britain still had no desire to see anything more than free trade in manufactures within Europe. If countries maintained their

[1] Robert Schuman, French foreign secretary for much of the ten years following the war.

individual tariffs against the outside world Britain could enjoy the benefits of free trade in Europe and continue to give preference to Commonwealth imports, but no prospect of liberalization in European trade was sufficient during the 1950's for Britain to think it worth submitting its own policies and laws to a European Executive Commission and Court. The Rome Treaty to establish the European Common Market was therefore signed in 1957 by the Six alone. Three years later Britain and the Scandinavian countries, Switzerland, Austria and Portugal, established the European Free Trade Area, with no further aims than to free trade in industrial goods between its members.[1]

The forms of international co-operation which developed in the years following the Second World War were therefore in some respects narrower than those planned by the Allies in 1944, although in others even more ambitious. The truly international institutions—IMF, IBRD and GATT—were bypassed for several years in favour of direct assistance from the US and special monetary and trade arrangements within Europe. Complete economic unification was agreed by six European countries, but at the expense of freer trade for the rest of the world; two new preferential trading blocs were established. Britain was severed from Europe, as was the US, and as the US balance of payments moved into permanent deficit at the end of the 1950's the Americans began to have some reason to regret their encouragement to the Europeans to discriminate against them. Nor did the Europeans continue entirely grateful for what had been done; as Professor Myrdal has pointed out, the only European countries which show no trace of anti-Americanism today are Switzerland, which received no Marshall Aid, and Sweden, which refused to take anything in the form of a gift.[2]

The other major international development of the 1950's was the realization that the capital requirements of the underdeveloped countries were far greater than had been envisaged at the end of the war. Indian independence now presented an important test case of whether a very poor underdeveloped country could grow

[1] The European Common Market and Free Trade Area will be more fully discussed in Chapter 13.

[2] Gunnar Myrdal, *Challenge to Affluence*, Gollancz, 1964.

at an acceptable rate without being under communist methods of control. The World Bank was clearly inadequate to constitute the main source of Western aid to underdeveloped countries; its funds were too limited and by its constitution it could only make loans according to the rules of 'sound' finance, i.e. which could confidently be expected to be repaid, and at market rates of interest. There were some international attempts to provide aid in more flexible forms; the UN Technical Assistance Board was set up in 1950, with small funds but with complete freedom to allocate them as it decided. In 1952 the proposal was first made of a Special United Nations Fund for Economic Development (SUNFED), to be supplied by the richer members of the UN with an annual $250 million to be distributed in the form of grants, and in which all members of the UN would have equal votes. This was opposed by the US and the UK, who preferred the weighted voting arrangements of the World Bank in which the rich countries have an automatic majority; they also feared a Soviet presence in an international aid organization. SUNFED was therefore never set up, though it continued to be debated for some years. Aid to the underdeveloped countries did increase, but on a national basis from government to government, with by far the greater part coming from the US.

THE INCREASING PROSPERITY OF THE DEVELOPED COUNTRIES

The aspect of the post-war scene which was to come as the greatest surprise to economists was, however, the rate of growth maintained by the majority of Western developed countries from the early 1950's onwards. When the war ended, economists and politicians had hoped that partly by means of the advance in knowledge of how to control economies brough about by Keynes' work and partly by means of a new degree of international co-operation, the pre-war experience of prolonged periods of depression and high unemployment might possibly be avoided. Once post-war reconstruction was over, it was expected that governments would need to operate the new economic techniques, stimulating demand at home by increased expenditure whenever unemployment rose towards an alarming height, and drawing upon international resources to solve balance of payments problems caused by declining exports.

In fact these techniques have hardly been needed, except to a certain extent in Britain and the US. The British economy grew by an average 2·6 per cent a year during the 1950's, and slowed down to a little over 2 per cent in the early 1960's, rates very similar to those achieved in the fifty years before the First World War. The American economy grew at much the same speed, although in this case it was appreciably less than the rates which prevailed early in the century. But both these performances seemed inadequate beside those of many of the other countries of Western Europe, which not only maintained high rates of growth after the reconstruction period was over and pre-war levels of output had been regained, but began to grow even faster still. Annual increases in national income of 4, 5, 6 or even 7 per cent were kept up by these countries throughout the 1950's and first half of the 1960's, and Japan showed an even more rapid development. Such high and sustained rates of growth had only been achieved in the pre-war years by the USSR, and Western economists had gradually come to believe with their Marxist counterparts that this kind of growth was only possible for an economy under authoritarian control, in which the government could enforce the annual re-investment of a very large proportion of national income. But the West had now begun to match Soviet levels of investment, while rapidly increasing levels of consumption at the same time; West Germany has been investing 25 per cent of its GNP since 1955, Japan over 30 per cent and France over 20 per cent, and even Britain and the US at least 17 per cent.

The governments of post-war Europe have not in these circumstances had to deal with problems of unemployment. Most of the countries of Northern Europe have had unemployment levels of under $2\frac{1}{2}$ per cent of the labour force since 1950; the main exception for some years was West Germany, which had to absorb 10 million refugees from the east, but by 1960 it too had ceased to have any substantial unemployment. It was indeed faced like most of these countries with labour shortages, both in the highly skilled and in the lowest paid occupations. The result has been an enormous international movement of labour—some half a million workers from the Commonwealth and colonies into the UK, and several hundreds of thousands of Algerians, Portuguese, Spaniards, southern Italians, Greeks, Turks and Yugoslavs into the northern half of the continent. Nor have Western governments been faced with declining exports; exports have been growing rapidly, and particularly those of the fastest growing economies. A more common problem, most acute for the UK, has been an even more rapid rise in imports.

Economists tend to differ as to whether this phenomenal rise in Western prosperity can continue for much longer. The more pessimistic school point out that there has been a slowing down in recent years in several of the fastest growing economies, notably the West German, and suggest that the relatively slow rate of growth achieved by the US is an example of what can be expected to happen once an economy has reached a very high level of consumer satisfaction. The optimists argue on the other hand that Western Europe's sustained growth is the result of new factors in domestic and international economic relations, and that these factors show every sign of permanency. The most important of these is the change in the economic role of governments. Although governments have not over the last twenty years needed on the whole to make the specific interventions to boost demand that Keynes had urged for the 1930's, their economic problems being more frequently the result of inflation than depression, they have nevertheless accepted the necessity for active participation and control. Their own share in demand and in investment[1] is now so large, even in the countries most committed to private enterprise, that it has a continuous sustaining effect on the levels of both; the confidence in the future felt by private consumers and businessmen which was once so important for economic activity now matters much less than it used to. The great development of social security systems in all European countries since the

[1] In Western countries the proportion of GNP attributable to government consumption ranges from 12 to 18 per cent. European governments are responsible for 40 to 60 per cent of all investment and even the North American governments for about a third.

war, the large nationalized sectors of industry, and the very large share of government in housebuilding, all appear to be permanent features of Western European economic life. Apart from this active participation in the economy, all governments have become accustomed to use taxation to encourage investment, and in particular investment in higher productivity, i.e. investment to increase output per man hour. Productivity in Europe has been rising faster than ever before, although it is still not as high as in the US; as governments are aware, it must continue to increase if high growth is to be maintained, since further growth in the European labour force can now only be slow. Most European governments have also begun in recent years to engage in long-term planning, previously only adopted by the French, and are thus further enlarging their economic responsibilities and further committing their economies to a sustained upward trend.

The other important factor which seems likely to maintain the growth of developed countries is the changed pattern and rapid expansion of world trade. A much larger proportion of world trade now consists of the exchange of manufactures for manufactures (see Chapter 3) between developed countries. Manufactures are becoming more and more sophisticated as technology advances and as consumers grow richer and their needs more diversified; the more rapidly products change, the greater the opportunities for exports. The rich countries no longer depend on an increase in incomes in primary producing countries for a rise in their exports, but can support each other's expansion into new fields of production. The modern increase in the volume of world trade, moreover, is partly attributable to the programme of liberalization begun in OEEC and carried on through the EEC, EFTA and most recently GATT; the cuts in tariffs and the abolition of quotas involved have been largely to the benefit of developed countries. Although the establishment of the EEC has appeared to divide the developed world by establishing a large preferential trading bloc within it, there remains a strong trend towards a more general international co-operation. The second half of the 1960's has already seen an agreement to reduce tariffs on industrial products through GATT, and a general revival of interest in the future of the IMF, apart from a change in the British attitude towards the EEC.

COMPETITION BETWEEN EAST AND WEST AND THE UNDERDEVELOPED COUNTRIES

The enormous growth in the national incomes of the developed countries of the West over the last twenty years has been distributed among their inhabitants on a relatively egalitarian basis. Substantial inequalities and pockets of severe poverty remain,[1] but in the eyes of the rest of the world the outstanding characteristics of the average inhabitant of the developed countries are his extraordinarily high standard of living and his wide possession of consumer goods. The advent of this almost general prosperity has brought about a great change in the relations between the West and the communist bloc, and between the West and the underdeveloped countries.

In the light of the experience of the last two decades, informed communists can no longer expect capitalism to collapse amid the disasters of over-production and the miseries of the working classes. Capitalism is now subject to a high degree of government control, even in a country like the US where production is still almost wholly the responsibility of private enterprise. Capitalist economies have shown themselves capable of sustaining the same high rates of investment and growth as communist economies; capitalist governments are turning increasingly to central planning as a means of maintaining and improving this state of affairs, and they have ceased to think high levels of unemployment or long or severe recessions politically tolerable. All these changes have tended to reduce the status of communist achievements; the West has managed to do the same things and has satisfied its consumers at the same time. The communist governments have consequently been forced to try to compete with the West on its own ground, and to give a new priority to improving average standards of living.

[1] See Chapter 15.

There were no changes in Soviet economic policy until after Stalin's death. At the end of the war the USSR embarked on a programme of tripling industrial production in 15 years, combined with continued heavy defence spending. At the time of the explosion of the first Soviet atomic bomb in 1949, the USSR manufactured less than one pair of shoes per citizen per year. Rents were kept low and medical care was free, but much of education had still to be paid for; severe labour legislation forbade unauthorized absence from work or change of job, and there was as great or more inequality in incomes as in many Western countries. By the time Stalin died in 1953 there had been great advances in industrial output; steel and coal were nearly twice the level of 1940, electricity generation had more than doubled and there were similar large increases in other sectors of heavy industry. Grain production, on the other hand, was little more than 10 per cent above the levels of the years before the First World War, with an additional 30 million people to feed. Under the Khruschev régime priorities suddenly changed. The government ceased to think so much of competing with the West in terms of armaments, and began to declare its intention to equal and overtake its standards of living within a generation. Khruschev's downfall was in fact partly due to his inability to fulfil such promises. During his years of power conditions did improve for Russian consumers. Minimum wages and pensions were increased and the highest salaries reduced, while the labour laws were relaxed; a much larger share of investment was directed to housebuilding, and there was a substantial increase in the production of consumer goods. But agricultural output rose slowly or declined, and sharply rising food prices cancelled out much of the higher incomes.

The policy of the present Soviet government, and that of the richer communist countries of Eastern Europe, continues nevertheless to be to make rapid improvements in standards of consumption. Living standards remain a long way behind the West; to give one example, the USSR produced a little over 200,000 passenger cars in 1965 and its target for 1972 is 700,000, while the US with its similar population already produces over 7 million a year. Agriculture in particular is extremely backward; the

38 million Russians still employed in agriculture produce less than their 7 million counterparts in the US. However, the change in priorities has come about, and has been accompanied by a profitable departure from dogma as regards planning methods and controls in the manufacturing sector, and this may yet happen in agriculture. Russian planners have since 1965 projected the same rate of growth for consumer goods as for the industrial sector, and average standards of living in the USSR and Eastern European countries are likely to begin to equal the West at least in the next generation. Meanwhile the communist governments are unlikely to allow social investment—in housing, education, health and public services in general—to advance more slowly than consumers' expenditure, so that their prosperity even while less than that of the West may well be established on a broader basis than in many Western countries.

Meanwhile for the last twenty years the underdeveloped countries have watched prosperity grow, both in the West and in the East, without seeing in most cases any substantial improvement in their own situation. In the course of the 1960's the terms of trade began to turn against primary producers. Commodity prices began to fall and the prices of manufactures to rise; the primary producers' exports became worth less and less per unit, while their imports cost more and more. Although aid from Western countries was rising steadily during the second half of the decade, and the USSR also now became one of the donors, these gains were largely wiped out by trade losses. Moreover the countries which had received the most aid—in many cases those with the best prospects of reaching an economic 'take-off' in the near future—were beginning to find a large proportion of their foreign exchange earnings mortgaged to interest and debt repayments.

Against the background of their own visibly increasing wealth, and with the added impetus provided by the Soviet entry into the field, the developed countries began to feel that more should be done for their neighbours. There was a revival in activity in international aid giving. The UN Special Fund was established in 1958 to assist with pre-investment projects—basic research and infrastructural investment which show no particular return themselves but without which a major investment in production is likely to be a failure. The World Bank began to lend to under-developed countries on a much larger scale, and was particularly active in contributing to India's Second Five Year Plan; its capital was doubled to $19 billion in 1959. A still more significant development was the establishment in the same year of the International Development Association (IDA), which unlike the Bank was given powers to lend at less than market rates of interest or at none, and to delay repayments for several years. IDA was however only provided with funds equivalent to less than half the Bank's lending resources, and it was placed under the Bank's control.

It was at this time, unfortunately, that the US, currently providing two-thirds of all government aid to underdeveloped countries and most of the funds for the World Bank, ran into the balance of payments difficulties which have remained a problem ever since. Imports rose above exports, while the outflow of American capital to overseas investment steadily increased. Fears of a future foreign exchange crisis reduced the willingness of the American administration to allow a further substantial rise in foreign aid. Other Western countries were urged to take a greater share of the burden, but the UK was faced with similar balance of payments difficulties, and France with the heavy cost of the Algerian war, while both these countries were in any case too heavily committed to assist their colonies and ex-colonies to feel able to make much larger contributions to multilateral aid programmes. The best hope was West Germany, and partly as a means of persuading her and other European countries to increase their contributions, the Development Assistance Group was organized on US initiative in 1959. Now, under the auspices of OECD, its members consist of the countries of Western Europe, North America and Japan, and its regular meetings help to co-ordinate national aid programmes.

The development of a conscience in the rest of the world about the problems of the underdeveloped countries has been an out-standing characteristic of the post-war years. Although against the background of world history it is remarkable that it should have happened at all, against the contemporary background of nationally and internationally declared intentions and resolutions little has in fact been done. The 1960's were declared the 'development decade'; its target was to raise the rate of growth of all underdeveloped countries to an average 5 per cent a year, which it was calculated would mean an average income per head in the underdeveloped world of $170 by 1970. It was hoped to achieve this by each developed country contributing in aid 1 per cent of its own Gross National Product per annum. In practice the actual contributions have so far (1966) averaged 0·6 per cent of the developed countries' GNP, although their own incomes have been growing by 4 to 5 per cent a year.

This gap between intentions and practice underlies the present relationship between the West and the underdeveloped world. The underdeveloped countries have become increasingly dissatisfied with the great and growing gap between their poverty and Western prosperity. They particularly resent the lower prices offered for their exports and their inability to break away from their extreme dependence on their trading partners; the ex-colonies are disillusioned by the lack of economic reality in their achievement of political independence. They see both the US and the USSR prepared to spend 10 per cent of their incomes on armaments, and most of the Western countries a not much smaller proportion, but not 1 per cent on assistance to them. At the same time the Western countries are felt to have exploited their poverty in the past and to be continuing to do so; it has been estimated that over the ten years since 1957 the change in the terms of trade has involved a gain to the industrialized countries of some $7,000 million a year from lower prices for their imports and a further gain of $3–4,000 million from higher prices for their exports, which would be the equivalent of the whole of Western aid according to its broadest possible definition. Communist financial assistance is still on a very small scale; Sino-Soviet aid in 1963 amounted to $0·4 million as against the US government's contribution of $3·7 million, but Russian commitments for the future are much larger. Moreover Russia has expanded her trade with underdeveloped countries more than seven times over the last decade, and China is following the same pattern.

PART THREE

WORLD ECONOMIC PROBLEMS— PROGRESS TOWARDS SOLUTIONS

CHAPTER TEN

The Outstanding Problems

The first part of this book gave a brief outline of the economic structure of the modern world, and the second part discussed the main trends in its development from the time of the first industrial revolution. In the course of these chapters the main specifically international economic problems which face the world today have already emerged. In the rest of this book, these problems will be looked at more closely, together with—where they exist—the beginnings of international solutions.

It will by now have become apparent that the outstanding characteristic of the modern economic world, and one which has been constantly reinforced by the trend of modern economic development, is the great discrepancy between the wealth of the different kinds of economies. In the years around the middle of this century, it gradually became accepted by the rich countries of the world that they had some responsibility for the economic advancement of the poor countries. In the generation since this decision was taken, however, the gap between the rich and the poor has in most cases continued to widen, and the major international economic problem has become how to help the underdeveloped countries to reach that stage in economic development at which growth can become a self-sustaining process, and can be maintained with no more outside help than that given by developed countries to each other. It has been realized simultaneously that the existing forms of world economic organization are inadequate to solve this problem, and that some of them may indeed help to perpetuate it.

The Western attitude to the underdeveloped world nevertheless remains ambiguous. Western countries are repelled by the political chaos frequent in the first years after independence, and by the nationalism from which they themselves have in many cases just begun to retreat. More important still, their leaders realize that Western prosperity depends increasingly on the trade of developed countries with each other, while their businessmen know that investment within the developed world is accompanied by far fewer risks than investment outside it. The power of the poor countries to do any direct damage to the rich is almost non-existent; with the important exception of China, they are not strong enough for outright aggression. Their prospects of economic warfare, through denying the developed countries the raw materials they export, are becoming increasingly limited as synthetic substitutes are developed for many commodities,[1] and such action would usually mean disaster for their own economies in any case. Why should the problems of the poor countries concern the rich at all?

The answer most often given to this question is a political one. In a world also divided between two very different political systems, the leaders of which both possess the weapons of total world destruction, the existence of such a cause for international jealousies and discontent must be a source of concern to the richer countries. Realistic politicians and economists in the West, whatever their theories of economic development at home, are aware that if the underdeveloped countries are to make any rapid progress towards development they must opt for a high degree of government economic intervention and control, and indeed except in China communist and Western methods of control have in recent years moved much closer together. Nevertheless there remains a real choice between communist and Western political systems, and the communist countries start with the advantage, as far as most underdeveloped countries are concerned, of never having been colonizing powers. (The USSR's record in what are now its own territories does not seem to apply.) Whatever Western countries may feel about the political aspects of this

---

[1] With the important exception so far of oil. But this is found in several different countries (see Chapter 2, p. 22), and even here patterns of fuel consumption could eventually change to the disadvantage of the oil-producing countries.

choice, it has its economic consequences for themselves. Communist economies, particularly those in the early stages of development, are inclined to place heavy restrictions on trade with the non-communist world. But whether or not some underdeveloped countries do choose communism, the economic prospects of a world in which all types of economies were embarked on steady growth would be very much brighter for the rich countries as well as the poor. This consideration, together with the fears of political conflicts arising from poverty, and with the modern development of a small but by no means negligible international concern for unnecessary suffering, has made the question of how to increase the standards of living of the underdeveloped countries a problem of world concern.

It is also a problem which is becoming increasingly urgent against a background of a very rapidly rising world population. The population of the world in 1800 has been estimated at a little under 1,000 million; it took a hundred years to increase to 1,600 million. But by 1950 it was nearly 2,500 million; by 1965 it was well over 3,000 million, having increased over these 15 years by almost the whole amount of the population of the pre-industrial world. By the year 2,000 it is expected to be over 6,000 million. According to the Food and Agriculture Organization nearly half the world's population is at present suffering from 'undernutrition or malnutrition, or both', i.e. is either starving or kept alive by a diet insufficiently balanced to maintain good health. In these circumstances the question of how and when the demand and supply of food—and in future space—can possibly be brought into balance takes on the proportions of a nightmare.

Modern advances in methods of birth control have certainly made it possible for this rate of increase to be slowed down. The worst problems of rising population are, however, concentrated in the underdeveloped economies. As prosperity increases, people tend to have fewer children. There are several possible reasons why this happens—the greater probability that children will survive to grow up, the greater difficulties involved in supporting extra children which paradoxically face the urban worker for a fixed wage more clearly than the poorer peasant, the desire to maintain and improve the new standards of living. In the developed countries of Europe and North America birth rates nearly all began a gradual decline in the last century which was continued until the 1930's, when they fell more sharply still in the years of depression. After a post-war rise in the 1940's and 1950's they have mostly tended to stabilize in the region of 17 to 23 per thousand (birth rates are measured in terms of the annual number of births per thousand of the population). Birth rates in the underdeveloped countries, however, are usually about twice as high as this; the average for Africa in recent years has been 47 per thousand, and the average for Asia 38. A recent United Nations report has observed that there is 'no readily measurable criterion . . . which distinguishes more sharply between more developed and less developed countries than the level of human fertility'. Unlike the other criteria, such as income levels, which may be used to distinguish the rich from the poor, birth rates are nearly always high or low, with very few countries recording intermediate levels. The only exceptions to the rule of high fertility in Asia, Latin America and Africa are Japan, which is now a developed country (and whose government undertook a major campaign to reduce the birth rate in the 1950's), Israel, Argentina and Uruguay, which are all economically advanced in relation to their neighbours, and the island of Zanzibar.

The underdeveloped countries also have very much higher death rates than those which prevail in the developed economies. Shortages of food, poor sanitary conditions and the lack of medical services mean that many people die young. A baby born in the USA or UK has an expectation of life of 67 years if a boy and 74 years if a girl; a baby born in Kenya has a life expectation of only 40 to 45 years. This means in practice that there are many deaths among children; for those children who survive to grow up, the chances of living to old age improve. However, the death rates of the underdeveloped countries have tended to fall in recent years, under the impact of public health measures and medical services which although inadequate are very much better than none at all. Death rates are no longer so high as to compensate for the high birth rates, so that the rate of population growth for the underdeveloped countries is much higher, in nearly all cases, than for the developed. The population of Western Europe and North America is increasing by about 1·5 per cent a year; the populations of most underdeveloped countries are rising by well over 2 per cent and sometimes as much as 3 per cent. These percentages sound small, but their implications over a generation are enormous. A country with a population of 50 million, for example, which increases by 1·5 per cent a year will have a population of 67 million twenty years later; if the increase is 2·5 per cent per annum, the population will be 82 million in twenty years. They also have severe implications for attempts to raise standards of living. A population increase of 3 per cent or more can easily cancel out almost the whole of the year's increase in national income; India's population grew between 1950 and 1962 by over 2 per cent a year, her national income by something over 3·5 per cent per annum and her income per head by an annual 1·5 per cent. If the population had remained stable, the increase in standards of living could have been well over twice as rapid.

The concentration of population problems in the underdeveloped economies means that resources are lacking—in terms of money and medical and administrative personnel—to solve them by artificial means, and, as in many developed economies, religious and social obstacles to such solutions still exist. These obstacles have also held back the development of international assistance for population control; the World Health Organization did not enter this field until 1965, and it was not until the end of 1966 that the UN General Assembly managed to agree that its agencies should 'assist when requested in further developing and strengthening national and regional facilities for training, research, information and advisory services in the field of population'. Attitudes are changing, particularly as the governments of the developed countries begin to realize that they have not inconsiderable population problems of their own. But although active government intervention can have spectacular results, as the Japanese experience in particular has shown, it is unlikely that it will take place on a large enough scale to make much difference to population growth over the next generation. The essential problem is still, at its least alarming extreme, how to help the populations of the underdeveloped economies to reach a standard of living at which their rate of increase will naturally slow down, and at its other extreme how to keep a large proportion of them alive at all.

Paradoxically, the basic answer to this problem is that the developed economies must grow richer still. Whatever the under-developed countries can do for themselves by making better use of their resources—and whether it is right for them to adopt Western or Eastern methods of organizing economic growth—they require enormous amounts of capital and skilled manpower if as a group they are to make any significant advance in the rest of this century. By far the greater part of the necessary capital can only come from the developed countries; the manpower must for at least another generation be provided or trained by them. Since it is not likely to be politically acceptable to make actual cuts in average standards of living in developed countries for the sake of the rest of the world, and nearly all aid costs the donor something,[1] the only hope is for the developed countries to maintain a high and steady rate of economic growth out of which they can con-tribute funds for overseas development without their own con-sumers feeling any loss.

This is not to say that there is not a considerable amount of reorganization of world economic arrangements which could be made—sometimes at little cost to any country—to the benefit of underdeveloped economies and often to the developed as well. Such prospects lie mainly in the field of international trade. It has been increasingly realized in recent years that the existing forms of government control over international trade, and also the post-war international agreements on the regulation of these controls, tend to work against underdeveloped economies. Nearly all reforms of international trade arrangements have been directed

[1] The main exception is in gifts of agricultural surpluses. Most Western countries have decided to protect and/or subsidize their farmers, even though some or all of their produce is at costs above world costs or can find no markets. They can therefore distribute such surpluses abroad at no extra cost to themselves other than those incurred in transport; the USA has done this on a large scale in recent years. It is however only a stop-gap form of aid, which does nothing to enable the recipient to improve its own productivity.

towards the ideal of free trade, but too many underdeveloped economies need to impose barriers against imports if they are ever to start their own industries going, and cannot afford to waste their available foreign exchange by allowing the import of large quantities of non-essential consumer goods. At the same time it is very important for them that the developed countries on which they depend for markets should not set up barriers against their own exports. Most developed countries are in fact relatively liberal in their trade policies relating to the import of raw materials and foodstuffs which they do not produce themselves, and tend not to impose tariffs on them unless they are favouring one group of underdeveloped countries at the expense of the rest. The exports of the underdeveloped countries consist at present mainly of such commodities, but if they are to improve their standards of living one obvious way to increase the value of their exports is to process some of these commodities themselves, and export them as manufactures or semi-manufactures. But in this case they are at once faced with substantial tariffs or quotas protecting the developed countries' own manufacturers. The principal international organization established to promote the liberalization of world trade, GATT, works basically on the principle of its members bargaining between each other to achieve a general cut in tariffs; the underdeveloped countries cannot afford to offer any concessions on their side. Moreover the most important area of free trade to be established since the war, the European Common Market, gave trading preferences to the ex-overseas territories of its members at the expense of all the other underdeveloped countries, who can only hope to obtain similar treatment in this huge market by offering concessions to EEC exports in exchange, and so losing any preferential arrangements they may already have elsewhere, as Commonwealth countries do with the UK.

One of the main difficulties for underdeveloped countries in taking action to improve world trading conditions for their products is that as they are to so great an extent in competition with each other; the temptation for each country to make the best bargain it can with its principal customers is considerable. But lack of co-operation between primary producers inevitably leads to over-production of primary commodities after a period of rising prices, followed by even sharper price falls once the surpluses reach the market. There is scope in these circumstances for the setting up of international commodity agreements to regulate production and prices. These were in fact one of the earliest forms of international economic co-operation; in the time of surplus between the wars the producers of sugar, wheat, tin, lead, rubber, steel, oil and zinc all managed to co-operate at least for a time to control their production, and shortly after the war agreements were made in which importers also joined with the object of securing stable prices or supplies. But these agreements have so far mainly been organized by developed countries, either in their role as primary producers (Canada, Australia and the USA for wheat) or as colonial powers or as importers. The underdeveloped countries have still to learn to co-operate between themselves to achieve these ends. There is however a new trend towards the emergence of the underdeveloped countries as a united economic pressure group. At the 1964 UN Conference on Trade and Development (UNCTAD) at Geneva, the underdeveloped countries took the other members by surprise in producing strong and unanimous objections to the trends and pattern of world trade, trade restrictions and preferences, existing international monetary arrangements and to the quantity and form of international aid. The Conference initiated a revision of the international arrangements relating to these subjects which has already had some results; these new ideas will be discussed in the following chapters.

At the same time, existing international arrangements relating to trade and monetary questions are not adequate for the developed countries themselves. While a considerable improvement on the pre-war situation, they are in need of enlargement and reform. When the present round of agreements to liberalize trade is completed, it will leave the developed world still sharply divided between the European Common Market—whatever its membership may finally turn out to be—and the rest. All developed countries, including the EEC as a whole, have reserved their agricultural production as something to be protected against the outside world despite the cost; there has been almost no progress towards freer trade in this respect, which involves a major waste of resources. International monetary arrangements have become increasingly makeshift in recent years; they have not allowed liquidity to expand automatically with the increase in the volume of world trade, and the two countries which supply the world's most used currencies, the USA and the UK, have found themselves in frequent balance of payments difficulties which slow down their expansion and hamper their exports of capital to the underdeveloped world. In these two countries in particular, and partly as a result of their currency problems, a proportion of the population remains impoverished amid the increasing wealth of the rest, constituting a severe blemish on the Western economic record.

CHAPTER ELEVEN

Aid to Underdeveloped Countries

WHY HAS AID BEEN GIVEN?

At the end of the 1950's there was a big jump in aid flows from the developed to the underdeveloped world. Within the space of three years, between 1959 and 1961, the net flow of official financial resources from OECD countries (Western Europe, North America and Japan) rose by over 40 per cent from $4·3 billion to $6·1 billion.[1] It then accounted for more than four-fifths of the world total.

Some of the political and economic factors behind this rise have been discussed in preceding chapters. Outstandingly, it was during these years that the massive colonial withdrawal really got under way. As the retreat gathered momentum, it needed only the gentlest nudge on the part of local nationalist leaders to persuade the foreign powers to pack up and go. In most cases timetables for developing the colonies' resources, both physical and human, to the point where independence could have some real meaning in terms of self reliance were completely abandoned; in some, such as the Belgian Congo (now Congo Kinshasa), such a timetable had never really existed, and the granting of independence was more like a panic-stricken scuttle than an orderly retreat. As a result, many of the new sovereign states which enrolled with the United Nations were of doubtful economic viability, even assuming that they had leaders capable of framing rational policies and administrators able to implement them. Moreover, the economic background against which independence was achieved was a gloomy one. The prices of many primary commodities, upon which the new countries depended for their

[1] A considerable amount of military aid flows from the more developed to the underdeveloped countries. This is not dealt with here.

income, and especially their foreign exchange income, had begun
to fall drastically. By contrast, the expectations of the peoples
concerned had been aroused during the campaigns for independence by nationalist leaders who sought support with promises of
unimpeded progress towards affluence once the colonialists had
gone. Finally, the Cold War was at this time still a major preoccupation of the two super powers, the USA and the USSR. In
geo-political terms decolonization seemed to leave empty spaces
in the world offering each power either a promise of expanded
influence abroad, or else a threat, if the other side were the first
to establish a commanding position.

The political and economic circumstances of the underdeveloped world thus brought a genuine need for assistance, while
demands for aid could be stated in a form calculated to bring a
swift reaction from the West, which in turn stimulated a counter-
response from the Communist bloc—though as we shall see
Communist aid has never reached more than a small fraction of
that originating in the West. It was the non-colonial Western
powers which led the big push as the colonialists retreated. The
USA, already in 1959 easily the biggest donor, increased its aid
by half; West German aid rose by nearly 90 per cent. Britain and
France on the other hand achieved increases of only 21 per cent
and 14 per cent respectively.

Perhaps inevitably, given such a rapid rise, there was a lack of
coherent aid strategy on the part of both donors and recipients.
The motives of the former and the expectations of the latter
became confused. In donor countries, enlightened long-term
political objectives—such as the promotion of political stability
through economic progress—were often overwhelmed by commercial interests or economic orthodoxy. In West Germany, for
instance, theoretically good aid policies were soon submerged in
the pursuit of export business for German industry; not only did
German society resist the costs of aid giving, but it insisted that
it should bring immediate and concrete benefits to West Germany.
In the USA, the administration's aid plans soon became restricted
by Congress' concern about budget deficits and the balance of
payments. Among the recipients, too, there was little idea as to
what sort of aid was required, from whom, or for what purpose.

As a result, much of the money received was spent irrationally, if not actually misappropriated. The very meaning of the word aid was obscured. In what sense is a credit at 10 per cent interest, repayable over five years, given to buy relatively expensive equipment from the donor, to be used on a doubtfully viable project, really aid? What sort of aid policy is it to extend largesse to countries with neither the will nor the ability to put it to proper use and to ignore those which could and would spend it productively? Can we describe as aid expenditure which, however generous its scale and terms, is aimed at promoting and protecting the predominant political, commercial and cultural influence of the donor and at maintaining the subservient client status of the recipient?

THE PATTERN OF AID-GIVING

To give these questions concrete reference, let us look first at the pattern of aid-giving of some of the main Western donors. Table 5 sets out the aid disbursed by the leading members of OECD in 1962/3. A comparison of the figures will bring out some of the main characteristics. The strongly commercial bias of West Germany's aid is indicated by the fact that two-thirds of the total was accounted for by loans, with a mere 12 per cent in the form of bilateral grants, i.e. gifts. The French figures are almost a mirror image of the German; nearly 80 per cent was in the form of grants, with lending only accounting for 13 per cent of the total. The French aid effort is also proportionately the greatest, the total being almost double that of Britain or West Germany, whose national incomes and average standards of living are broadly comparable. At this time French aid accounted for well over 1 per cent of France's gross national income. The corresponding proportions for Britain and the USA were about one-half of 1 per cent, and for West Germany about one-third of 1 per cent.

France again stands out as an enlightened donor if we look at the way in which bilateral aid is provided. Table 6 shows bilateral aid commitments by end use.

It can be seen that a relatively high proportion of French funds

TABLE 5
Aid* disbursed from OECD: 1962/3 average ($ million)

	All OECD	USA	France	UK	W.Germany
Bilateral†					
Grants	2,532	1,362	727	211	54
Reparations	149	—	—	—	70
Loans repayable in local currencies	360	360	—	—	—
Sales for local currencies	930	928	—	—	2
Gross lending‡	2,054	1,035	159	201	303
Amortization	− 502	− 240	− 38	− 36	− 56
Total	5,523	3,445	848	375	373
Multilateral‖					
Grants and capital subscriptions	516	218	72	42	68
Bond purchase (net)‡	4	—	—	—	− 4
Total	522	218	72	42	64
Grand total (net)§	6,043	3,663	919	417	436

* Strictly speaking, this should read 'Flow of public long-term financial resources to developing countries'.
† i.e. aid given directly by one country to another, as opposed to 'multilateral' aid given by donor countries acting in consortia, usually through a permanent international organization.
‡ For more than one year.
‖ Including others.
§ Totals are inclusive of other small items.
Source: OECD: *The Flow of Financial Resources to Less Developed Countries, 1956–63*, Paris, 1964.

provided for capital projects went to agriculture, for almost all underdeveloped countries the most important sector and the one most difficult to develop. Another large share went to current expenditure and to technical co-operation. The virtue of this distribution perhaps needs explanation. Until recently it was a widely held view that the developing countries' main problem was a shortage of capital and that accelerated development simply required increased expenditure on capital account. Since in the great majority of underdeveloped countries the rate of saving was

TABLE 6

Official Bilateral Commitments: 1962/3 Average

	Total OECD		USA		France		UK	
	$ m	%	$ m	%	$ m	%	$ m	%
Capital projects	2,368	33·5	1,136	26·1	427	48·2	177	34·1
of which								
agriculture, forestry, fishing	246	10·3	114	10·1	66	15·4	26	14·6
transport and communications	504	21·2	244	21·5	70	16·3	23	12·9
energy	488	20·6	273	24·0	68	15·9	23	12·9
Indus basin	48	2·0	30	2·6	—		2	1·2
industry	597	25·2	259	22·7	33	7·7	55	31·1
social infrastructure	457	19·2	216	19·0	189	44·2	27	15·3
other	28	1·1	—	—	—	—	20	11·2
Specified current expenditure	205	2·9	20	0·4	172	19·4	9	1·8
Non-project assistance	3,177	45·2	2,696	62·0	—	—	243	46·8
of which import finance	2,782	87·5	2,561	94·9	—	—	89	36·7
Technical co-operation	896	12·7	406	9·3	276	31·2	75	14·4
Total (including others)	7,026		4,344		885		519	

Source: OECD, ibid.

insufficient to bring this about, it was held that the main job of aid was to fill the gap between the actual rate of savings and some theoretically 'correct' rate of capital expenditure. Capital expenditure is of course important, but it is of little use to spend large amounts of money on dams and irrigation canals, for example, if there is no one to teach the farmers the sophisticated techniques of irrigated cultivation. This example is not academic; a case is on record of the commissioning of a large irrigation dam, the completion of which was followed by peasant riots when the farmers woke up to find their fields flooded and their crops ruined. Nor is it helpful to tie funds to investment in new manufacturing capacity when existing plants are working at far below the optimum rate because they cannot get foreign exchange to import the necessary raw materials and spares. Despite such experiences, the equation of conventionally defined capital expenditure with 'development' expenditure has shown a remarkable persistence, both among donors and recipients. Among the various possible explanations of this intellectual inertia there are three which deserve special mention. The first large-scale experience of aid giving was that extended by the USA to Europe after the war under the Marshall Plan. The problem then was largely one of restoring the capital stock—the factories, communications, power stations etc.—which had been destroyed, in order to provide an already skilled and experienced labour force with the physical facilities it needed. This pattern of assistance was adopted uncritically and irrelevantly when the recipients changed to underdeveloped countries. The second reason for the emphasis donors place on capital projects is simpler; they show. It is easier for purposes of propaganda to point to a hotel or a power station than to an agricultural credit programme. The third point is that many donors cannot refrain from exacting a commercial return from their aid. They like the funds they provide to be used for the purchase of their own goods, and it has proved easier to achieve this for capital projects requiring identifiable machinery and equipment.

If we now look at Table 7, which shows how the main donors distribute their aid, the French aid effort appears in clearer perspective. Nearly 95 per cent went to French-speaking countries, principally in Africa. It is quite plain that French aid is an important element in France's overall aim to preserve its traditional areas of influence. From an international point of view this may be criticized. There is little doubt that much of the aid France extends to its ex-colonies could be used to better effect elsewhere. Against this it must be said that the scale and type of aid it gives is such as to make a significant impact on the countries concerned, which is by no means always true of Western aid in other parts of the world. The French moreover distribute their aid fairly rationally between the countries they give it to, which is not a characteristic of the other major donors' aid programmes. For instance, Table 7 shows that American aid to South Korea,

TABLE 7

Principal Donors and Recipients of Net Bilateral Aid: 1962/3 Average

	$ million	% of total
Given by the USA; total	3,445	
of which India received	638	18·6
Pakistan received	356	10·3
S. Korea received	237	6·8
Turkey received	194	5·6
S. Vietnam received	184	5·1
Given by France; total	848	
of which Algeria received	308	36·3
African and Malagasy States received	291	34·3
Overseas Departments and territories received	146	17·3
Morocco and Tunisia received	59	7·0
Given by the UK; total	375	
of which India received	61	16·2
Kenya, Uganda and Tanganyika received	102	27·2
Pakistan received	21	5·6
Given by West Germany*; total	373	
of which Israel received	64	17·1
India received	49	13·1
Liberia received	33	8·8
Pakistan received	31	8·3
Turkey received	26	6·9
Chile received	19	5·0

* All grants; West German grants to other countries totalled $75 million.
Source: OECD, ibid.

Turkey and South Vietnam, whose combined populations total some 76 million, nearly equalled that to India with a population more than six times as large. The British figures show that Kenya, Uganda and Tanganyika (now Tanzania), with a mere six per cent of India's population, received over one and a half times as much aid. Again, West German aid to India was only 50 per cent higher than that to Liberia, although India has at least 400 times as many people. The relative meanness of aid to India is but one of the many anomalies in the distribution of Western aid.

The following quotation from a recently published analysis of aid,[1] the findings of which have been extensively used in this chapter, succinctly describes the main criteria which seems in fact to have determined the distribution of aid. 'Given that a country is regarded by the Western world as "developing", and that it is not closely attached to Moscow or Peking, there seems, on the evidence, to be three main alternative ways in which it can qualify for a large amount of aid per head. First, it should be closely attached to France, preferably as an overseas department, but failing that as a member of the franc zone. Second, it should have a common border with one of the communist countries, or be thought by America to be in immediate danger from communism, or tolerate American bases. Thirdly, like Algeria and Liberia, it should have some newly discovered resource of interest to foreign business.' To this list of irrational political, historical and commercial factors which in practice seem to determine how much of the world aid total an individual underdeveloped country may expect, a fourth factor may be added; other things being equal, it is much better to be a small country than a large one. The authors of *International Aid* have compiled an interesting table of the main recipients of aid, ranked according to how much they get per head of the population.[2] Out of a list of 26 countries or groups of countries, the ten at the bottom of the table in terms of grant-aid per head accounted for more than 80 per cent of the total population. The average population of the countries at the top of the table was around 14 million; that of the ten which received least aid per head was some 85 million. The implications for the majority of the people of the underdeveloped countries are serious.

Finally, we must consider aid from the Sino-Soviet bloc and from international agencies. Even taken together, aid from these sources is small in relation to the world total. Aid *commitments* from the Eastern bloc amounted to $425 million in 1963, a mere 7 per cent of the OECD total. Moreover, this figure bears little relation to Sino-Soviet aid *spending*, since for one reason or

[1] I. D. Little and J. M. Clifford, *International Aid*, George Allen & Unwin, 1965.
[2] Ibid., p. 68.

another there are usually long delays between offers of aid from the Eastern bloc and the actual use of such aid. Underdeveloped countries which speak hopefully of balancing aid from East and West should note that any literal attempt to do this would almost certainly result in a reduction of their total aid receipts. Looking at what sort of aid the communist countries give and to whom, it is evident that they have no clearer economic rationale than the Western aid givers, and probably rather less.

Of the international agencies, the most important are the World Bank (see Chapter 9, pp. 103, 104), and its two affiliates, the International Development Association and the International Finance Corporation. All are special agencies of the UN. The policies of the World Bank may be criticized in detail, but of all aid sources it is the one which makes the most effort to combine a fair and economically justifiable distribution of aid between countries with a reasonably rational appreciation of the economic priorities within each country. Unfortunately its resources are small—none of the Eastern bloc participate in its financing—and the average of $365 million which it provided to the under-developed world in 1961 and 1963 was only just over a tenth of bilateral aid from the USA.

Other United Nations' aid falls mainly under the head of technical assistance, and averaged well under $200 million in 1962/3. By no means all of it is for economic development, strictly defined, and may indeed at times conflict with economic priorities.

THE VALUE OF FOREIGN AID

So far we have described some of the main aspects of aid-giving, with comments and criticisms which are intended as signposts towards a more general understanding of questions of principle. The most important of these questions is: what does it mean to give aid? This has been touched on earlier in the chapter, but up to now the word has been used loosely and it has been accepted that what donors call aid is correctly described as such. In a more precise form, the question is: what does it cost donors to give aid, and how does it benefit recipients? Strictly speaking the cost to the donor of a given amount of aid should be its full face value. Every £ of aid should involve the sacrifice of an equivalent amount of resources. This would mean that donors should not require any repayment nor expect any interest. Nor should they insist on the tying of such aid to the purchase of their own industries' goods. The supply of such goods only involves a sacrifice if the full capacity of the industry concerned would otherwise have been employed as a result of normal commercial demand. There is reason to believe that in some cases so-called aid is more than recovered in terms of orders for the donor's industries. On the other side it may be argued that individual recipient countries are less interested in whether or not donors are sacrificing something than in whether or not what is offered them helps them. But underdeveloped countries have a collective interest in encouraging greater generosity among donors. There is no objection to the donors giving assistance which costs them nothing, but real generosity means readiness to make a sacrifice, and they should not be allowed to delude themselves that they can fulfil their responsibilities (or realize their interests) without cost.

Moreover, in most cases donors manage to avoid the full costs of aid-giving only at the expense of the recipients. The two main methods of passing on the cost have already been mentioned; requiring repayment with interest, and tying the funds supplied to the donors' own industry. The 'respectable' reason for insisting on these terms is the protection of the donors' balance of payments, though there is also often an element of sheer commercial self-interest. The question of repayments has now become a matter of great importance with the dramatic rise in the public debt burden of the underdeveloped countries from some $10 billion in 1957 to an estimated $45 billion ten years later. With the level of world aid static or declining, there has been a significant fall in the net value of aid, i.e. aid net of repayments and interest to donors, and unless the trend is reversed the net benefits of world aid to underdeveloped countries will eventually fall to zero. Some donor countries have much to answer for in bringing this situation about. Officials in underdeveloped countries have often not had great powers of financial discrimination, and there is no doubt that in some cases they have been persuaded to accept fairly hard commercial deals as aid, thus laying the basis of a formidable debt problem, which in turn mars the reputation of their country among donors and may even lead to the choking off of aid itself. Donors have no excuse for this. If they are genuine aid givers, part of their responsibility must lie in educating the recipients about what is involved in the terms offered, and in satisfying themselves that the terms can be met. One organization which is very scrupulous about this is the World Bank. The terms of its lending may not always be ideally generous, but it takes great pains to ensure that the projects it finances will generate enough extra income to enable its loans to be repaid.

The second method of passing on the cost—aid-tying—is in many ways even more burdensome to recipients. There are two main forms, project tying and procurement tying. The first means that the aid can only be used for specific, defined projects; the second that it must be spent on goods from the donor country. Many donors insist on both conditions, and much aid is both project and procurement tied. The disadvantage of project tying is that it tends to result in distortions in the recipient's economy. Most noticeable is a less than full employment of the recipient's indigenous resources. In India, where foreign exchange has been chronically short for a decade or more, project tying has led to the continuous creation of new productive capacity, despite the fact that existing enterprises can only work at half speed, because they cannot obtain the foreign exchange necessary to import essential raw materials, spares etc. In other countries, particularly in Africa, where the financial structure is relatively underdeveloped, project tying brings to light a local cost problem. This means that the recipient government simply cannot find the money to finance the domestic costs of a project. Since donors have in the past been willing to provide only the foreign exchange costs of project tied aid, this has meant that materials etc. for the project which could in fact have been supplied locally, have been imported instead, again resulting in under-utilization of domestic resources.

The clearest disadvantage of procurement tying is that the

recipient cannot buy its imports in the cheapest market. This is not always just a matter of the donor's goods being marginally more expensive than those available elsewhere; in the case of specialized equipment there may be virtually no competition between suppliers in the donor country, a situation which is often ruthlessly exploited, resulting in prices up to 50 per cent higher than those ruling in normal export markets. Another less important, but still significant, drawback for recipients is the administrative effort which is required to give effect to the obligation to import only from the donor by ensuring that even the smallest items are purchased from suppliers in the donor country.

The worst aspects of procurement tying are found when it is conjoined with project tying. There are, however, two special cases where procurement tying results in much less severe extra costs to the recipients, and may even be free from them. The first is the case of commodity aid. The bulk of this is accounted for by food aid from the USA. American food surpluses are not produced primarily to give to underdeveloped countries, but result from a domestic political decision to protect and subsidize the American farmer. There is therefore little real sacrifice involved for the donor in giving it away, since the US government would otherwise incur the costs of storing, destroying or disposing of it in some other way. But if there is little or no cost to the USA, this is also true for the recipients, though it should be noted that such aid may not be in the long term interest of a recipient country, in the sense that it may discourage the development of its own domestic agriculture and reduce the incentive for effective birth control programmes. It may also be harmful to some underdeveloped countries, such as Thailand or Burma, whose export markets are thereby curtailed. Nevertheless it is of course better and more rational for the food to be given to countries that need it than for it to be destroyed, which is what happened in the 1930's.

The second special case of procurement tying is tied technical assistance. The importance of this form of aid has already been stressed; in many underdeveloped countries the critical scarce resource is not money, but trained technical and professional staff capable of designing a sensible development strategy and of arranging and implementing the policies and programmes to carry it through. The main argument in favour of tied technical assistance is that the necessary skills and training programmes can best (and perhaps only) be supplied by donor governments. Individual donor governments are in the best position to obtain the most appropriate people or organization to carry out this work. The main disadvantage of tied technical assistance would probably be unavoidable even if it were untied or internationalized. It arises when there are a number of donors interested in a particular underdeveloped country. Donors are often more or less hostile to each other, and this hostility is reflected in the personnel they supply, and even where they are not, differences in political, cultural and linguistic backgrounds may lead to basic disagreements and misunderstandings between the experts, bringing as much trouble as help to the recipient government. This situation is naturally at its worst when as sometimes happens the experts have clearly been provided in order to further the commercial advantage of the aid-giver.

These criticisms of the terms of aid and the methods by which immediate advantage is sought or costs passed on should not be overstressed. It would be as unexpected to find perfect enlightenment in the field of aid as it would in any other field of human endeavour. Moreover progress has been made, at least so far as Western aid-givers are concerned, in co-operation to improve the terms of aid and to reduce the ill effects of aid tying. This has gone hand in hand with greatly increased efforts to tailor the aid offered to the actual requirements of underdeveloped countries, with much more careful study of these requirements.

While a more rational and professional approach to aid-giving is developing, however, this has been offset since 1962/3 by a reluctance to increase the amounts spent on aid, or even to maintain them at 1962/3 levels. This is especially obvious in the USA, where the President's annual aid requests have been savaged by Congress. Compared with the $4·3 billion average committed in 1962/3, Congress approved a mere $2·3 billion in 1968, which was a cut of $1 billion from the total proposed by the President, and the lowest aid appropriation since the Marshall Plan was launched twenty years before. There are numerous reasons for the increasing meanness of the richest country the world has ever known. One of the most important is a disenchantment with the results aid has shown in the past, both in terms of progress brought about in recipient countries, and in terms of 'buying friendship' for the USA. This has been followed by the huge foreign exchange burden of financing what most Americans felt ought to have been a small, cheap war in Vietnam. Associated with both of these is an increasingly strong current of isolationism. Better relations with the USSR have meanwhile reduced the competitive aspects of aid-giving, while a steady deterioration in the balance of payments has also contributed, though probably least of all.

Unfortunately, some underdeveloped countries seem to be doing all they can to promote these undesirable undercurrents in the USA and elsewhere by the stridency of their criticisms of Western aid policies. In 1967 all the underdeveloped countries met in Algiers in preparation for the next UNCTAD[1] meeting, to discuss how to persuade the rich half of the world to continue and increase its help. There they were addressed by their host, Colonel Boumedienne, the Algerian President, in the following terms: 'The advanced countries are veritable octopi, whose tentacles are drawing ever tighter on the developing world . . . we should consider whatever contribution the industrialized countries make as a simple restitution of a tiny part of the debt the Western countries contracted by their odious exploitation.' There are elements of truth in such statements, but they are hardly likely to be recognized by the majority of the people in aid-giving countries, and will breed truculence rather than sympathy. While enlightened governments may be able to increase the aid they give against the background of an indifferent public opinion, they cannot do so when the electorate is actually hostile.

What of the future? The key to it lies in the United States. It is far too early to say that enlightened long-term policies will yield to prejudice or to narrow, immediate self-interest. Progress is being made towards more rational arrangements for the provision of world liquidity[2] which should take some of the pressure off the USA, as well as other major donors like the UK. Much more

---

[1] See p. 128.   [2] See Chapter 14.

thought is also being devoted to how given amounts of aid can make the maximum possible contribution to development. For these reasons, if there is a recovery in the will to help the poor countries of the world, aid should make a very much more useful contribution than it has in the past.

CHAPTER TWELVE

The Liberalization of World Trade

The years since the Second World War have been a time of considerable change in world trading arrangements. There has been a general dismantling of physical controls on trade—i.e. of direct prohibitions of imports or the limitation of imports within fixed quotas—and a general lowering of tariffs. There has also been a new trend towards the establishment of trading blocs, within which the members abolish restrictions on trade with each other while retaining barriers against the rest of the world. As far as the developed countries are concerned, the two main new trade groups to have been founded since the war, the EEC and EFTA, together with the general negotiations to reduce barriers to trade carried out through GATT, have resulted in a high degree of liberalization of trade between them.

These countries' already enormous share of world trade has as we saw in Chapter 3 maintained a rapid rise over the last two decades. This has not been the case for the trade of the underdeveloped world, and the main problem for the future remains the trading arrangements for underdeveloped countries, both between themselves and with developed trading partners. The question of reforming these arrangements is complicated by the fact that it is argued on the one hand that recent reforms in world trade rules have led to very little liberalization as far as the exports of the underdeveloped countries are concerned, and may indeed in some cases have increased protection against them, and on the other that a general move to liberalization is unsuitable for the problems of the underdeveloped countries, who must continue to protect their own developing industries and precarious trading balances for many years to come. Before going on to consider the possibilities of helping these countries by means of new international trade arrangements, however, it will be useful to look more closely at the main changes which have been organized in the developed world.

THE EUROPEAN TRADING BLOCS

'We are supporters of the European Economic Community, and not of the Common Market. The Common Market is one means among many of creating the EEC. The Community can only be established through the drawing up of rules for a common economic policy . . . through the harmonization of social legislation, through the elaboration of a genuine common agricultural policy, through the co-ordination of credit policy, through effective control of cartels and monopolies. . . . To reach these goals, we shall have to merge the three executives of EURATOM, ECSC and EEC into one and endow the new body with progressively increasing powers until it is in a position to develop a common economic policy leading on ultimately to a common foreign and military policy; the European executive must be responsible to a Parliament elected by universal suffrage.'

This extract from a speech made to the European Assembly in 1961 by the French statesman André Philip is a useful outline of the meaning of economic integration to the founders of the EEC, and also a reminder that to many of its originators political objectives were at least as important as their economic aims. For the true 'European' the goals described by André Philip remain unchanged. During the first ten years of its existence, however, the Community's progress towards unification has been mainly limited to a small area of economic achievement; full economic integration remains distant, and political integration more distant still.

The EEC's greatest success has been in the tariff cutting programme laid down in the Rome Treaty, which the members have twice agreed to speed up; internal tariffs thereupon disappeared in July 1968, eighteen months earlier than originally envisaged. A common market in agricultural products is also due to start functioning then, agreement having finally been reached after several years' wrangling on the unification of farm support programmes. While these are major achievements, there have been few others. National differences in tax and social security systems constitute a substantial barrier to full economic integration, in particular to the free movement of capital and enterprise. No progress has, however, been made towards harmonizing the six social security systems; the only important international activity in the social security field continues to be that of the ECSC, which has been spending an annual £4 to 5 million on retraining and resettling redundant miners, although member countries have also guaranteed equal status in their own social security schemes for all Community nationals employed. It has been agreed in principle that all countries should adopt the French type of 'value-added'[1] turnover tax, but there is still considerable opposition to this, since it is not in any sense a socially redistributive tax system, being paid indiscriminately by all consumers; the Netherlands in particular has previously avoided taxing food and other basic essentials. Finally, there is little sign of a common economic policy, not even in individual sectors such as transport or power, although February 1967 may have seen a breakthrough in this respect since a five year 'economic programme' constituting a limited form of planning was at last agreed upon.

Political progress towards true integration has of course been held back by the change in French attitudes under the rule of General de Gaulle. The Rome Treaty was itself much more cautious in establishing a supra-national form of government than the previous treaty setting up the ECSC; the Common Market was given a Council of Ministers responsible to their own governments, assisted by an independent Commission of nine members appointed for four years and forbidden to accept or seek instruction from outside. The Commission's decisions are taken by majority vote and it is only accountable to the European Assembly; the Council's decisions were, however, to be unanimous for the first eight years, after which the Treaty made provision for a gradual progress towards majority rule once the

[1] A form of purchase tax which is levied at each stage of manufacture or distribution at which an article becomes more valuable; the final accumulation of tax naturally appears in the final price to the consumer.

transition period was over. This is the crucial area of surrender of national sovereignty, in which the supporters of the Common Market divide into different parties—the true European federalists, who believe in complete political and economic integration, and those whose interests are purely economic, but who are themselves divided between those who see the Common Market as a means of establishing as wide an area of free trade as possible, and those who see it as a means of protecting Europe against the rest of the world. The diverse interests in the latter group have found themselves assisted by de Gaulle, whose vague but anti-federalist concept of '*l'Europe des Patries*' can be used as a description of many different forms of a semi-united Europe. In 1965 de Gaulle launched an attack on the powers of the Commission, and at the same time campaigned for an abandonment of majority decisions by the Council on 'vitally important' matters. In the prolonged dispute which followed he had some success in reducing the powers of the Commission in relation to the Council, but the other five members have continued to refuse to accept any alteration in the Council's voting arrangements, while the French have made it clear that they will not in fact accept any majority decision they believe to be contrary to their interests.

Against this background of dispute on such basic questions the political development of the EEC has naturally been slow. As a result, it is still without a common policy over such matters as trade with Eastern Europe or with the underdeveloped world as a whole, although treaties of association have been signed with Greece, Turkey and Nigeria. Britain's attempt to join the Common Market in 1963 was blocked by France, although all the other members would on the whole have welcomed British entry; Despite their support it happened again in 1967 when Britain, together with Denmark, Norway and Ireland, made a new application. The one identifiable item of political progress towards unification has been the merger with the Community, in July 1967, of the ECSC and EURATOM; all three bodies are now ruled by one Executive Commission. However, it may well be that political progress should not be measured as yet by results; it is often argued that the last ten years have seen a great change in the attitude of the average Community voter towards his membership of a united Europe, and that the experience in working together built up by the politicians and civil servants is one of the most important guarantees of future advance towards true unification. Whatever the degree of progress by the EEC towards its own goals, its existence and development has been of considerable significance to the rest of the world in several respects. In the first place, it has advertised the value of economic integration. Some economists argue that the main theoretical advantage of free trade—freedom to specialize in the most efficient forms of production and to benefit from the economies of scale involved in producing for a mass market—have not applied to the EEC, where natural resources do not differ significantly from country to country and in which all members already had access to markets quite large enough to support the great majority of modern industries. The other main advantage cited for integration, the increased competition, stimulating firms to greater efficiency and eliminating the least capable, is also not a necessary consequence, particularly as the EEC is not equipped with the detailed legislation and the tradition of government action against price-fixing by cartels which exist in the USA and now in the UK. However, although the spectacular growth of the European economies had begun before the Rome Treaty came into effect, it has been maintained and accelerated since, and intra-Community trade increased between 1958 and 1966 by the undeniably large proportion of 238 per cent. One of the most important effects of integration has probably been the confidence in future growth sustained in Community businessmen, with its obvious effect on programmes of investment. Third countries are inevitably attracted by such results, as the reversal of the attitude to membership of British governments of both parties has shown.

At the same time, the formation of the EEC has compelled the rest of the world, and in particular the underdeveloped countries, to give new attention to the dangers of modern forms of protection in international trade. The signatories to the Rome Treaty included both high and low tariff countries. The original plans for the common external tariff pointed to one which would in practice be rather higher on average than the existing individual patterns. This was in fact modified to a lower level, but could not of course prevent there being many cases of exporters from out-side the Community being faced with increased barriers to trade with the originally low-tariff countries. Before 1957, only France gave preferences on imports of tropical agricultural imports in favour of her overseas territories. With the formation of the EEC, all members agreed to give such preferences to the products of the present or former dependencies of France, Belgium, Italy and the Netherlands, with the result that all the remaining countries of Africa and Asia, and the whole of Latin America, found them-selves faced with European tariffs against such exports as coffee or cocoa, while the products of their competitors in EEC ex-colonies are admitted duty free. The Community held out the prospect of treaties of association for affected tropical producers, but so far only one—with Nigeria—has been signed, and this demonstrated the necessity for the associating country to offer preferences in exchange which it could ill afford.

The other important trend to increased protection brought about by the foundation of the EEC is in agriculture. Within the EEC, as much as a quarter of the active population is still engaged in agriculture, and this includes some of the most inefficient farming in the developed world. More than two-thirds of the farms are less than 25 acres in size—the average for Italy is 5½—which may be compared with the average for England and Wales of 85 acres. Although there are considerable variations within Europe, European farm costs tend to be far higher than those of the big grain and meat producers of North America, Australia and New Zealand. The members of the EEC, like most developed countries, have been in the habit of protecting their uneconomic farmers against cheaper imported foods. The reasons for this vary; in some countries it is partly explained by the importance of the agricultural vote, elsewhere by a (now outdated) belief in the importance of self-sufficiency in food in time of war, or by social and perhaps sentimental considerations. One valid social consideration is that unless farmers do receive some degree of protection from their government the standards of living of the agricultural community never tend to improve; the competition in the production of the 'temperate' foodstuffs grown in most de-veloped countries is such that increases in productivity normally result in lower prices rather than higher profits and wages. EEC members have been accustomed to protect their farmers by means of levies on imports, quantitative import controls and tariffs, resulting in artificially high food prices even where, as in West Germany, a substantial proportion of food is imported from other countries, including wheat from the USA. The introduction of a unified European market for agricultural products, with uniform price support, will almost inevitably result in greater self-sufficiency in food within the EEC than has previously been the case; French food surpluses in particular will tend to replace the West German imports from overseas. Further problems will arise if Britain becomes a member, since the British system of farm protection is to subsidize farmers directly from general taxation while allowing in imports of food (mainly from the Commonwealth) duty free or at very low tariffs. The British consumer consequently pays world market prices and enjoys a lower cost of living, and since Britain produces a smaller proportion of its food, and on average more efficiently, than is the case in the EEC, the burden in taxation is not excessive (as it would be if this system were introduced on the Continent). But if the EEC system were extended to Britain, several new import barriers would rise against the outside world, together with British food prices.

In the agricultural sector, therefore, the establishment of the EEC does not encourage a more efficient utilization of world economic resources. The countries which tend as a result to be faced with higher barriers against their exports are in fact mainly other developed countries, in particular the USA, Canada, Australia and New Zealand, who are the biggest and commonly the most efficient producers of the kinds of foodstuffs consumed in Europe. Nevertheless some underdeveloped countries are concerned, and the underdeveloped world could be increasingly affected in the future by the discouragement to the development of new food production aimed at European markets. Moreover any misuse of resources in the developed world means a reduction in wealth with which to assist the rest.

The other major new trading bloc, the European Free Trade Area, does not incur the same criticisms from the outside world as the EEC. It has been as successful as the EEC in carrying out its tariff cutting programme, having taken six years to remove quotas and tariffs from industrial products instead of the $9\frac{1}{2}$ originally planned, and intra-EFTA trade, though not increasing as rapidly as trade within the EEC, more than doubled between 1960 and 1966. The smooth implementation of the EFTA programme and the lack of disputes between the members have of course been largely due to its limitation to purely economic objectives, but such freedom from trouble nevertheless came as a surprise in view of the extra difficulty involved in establishing a free trade area—which has no common external tariff—through the necessity of proving the country of origin of imports and in some cases of their constituent parts (according to EFTA rules a product counts as originating from a member country provided that materials from outside the area used in making it are not worth more than 50 per cent of its export price). While a free trade area is less potentially economically efficient than a full customs union, mainly for the reason that a relatively inefficient firm in a low tariff country may have a decisive cost advantage over a more efficient competitor in a high tariff country, EFTA has made a substantial contribution to trade among its members without increasing any barriers to trade against the outside world.

GATT AND THE KENNEDY ROUND

Another consequence of the establishment of the EEC was to give new emphasis, for non-members, to the importance of negotiations for general tariff cuts under the auspices of GATT. One such round of negotiations—the Dillon round of 1962—resulted in agreement on a general cut of 20 per cent on industrial products, which meant that the EEC's final common external tariff was reduced to an average indisputably lower than that of the previous individual tariffs. Without the possibility of further progress under GATT, the protectionist aspects of the EEC would have caused much greater concern to the other developed countries. As it was, the USA had become sufficiently disturbed by 1962 about the way in which the Common Market was developing to pass the US Trade Expansion Act, which was aimed at broadening the area of free trade to include the other developed countries, especially Britain and the USA, at including agricultural products (which the USA itself had previously insisted on excluding from GATT discussions), and at reducing barriers to exports from underdeveloped countries. The Act empowered the US government to offer to negotiate tariff cuts of up to 100 per cent on all commodities of which exports by the USA and the members of the EEC combined constituted 80 per cent or more of world trade, and cuts of up to 50 per cent on the rest. It was hoped by this means to encourage both the British government and the government of the Six to negotiate British membership of the EEC, since with Britain included there would be a possible 25 main commodity groups qualifying for the 100 per cent cut, and without Britain only two. The Act also allowed the US government to eliminate tariffs on tropical agricultural and forest products if the CM members would do the same.

Since Britain did not join the CM, the 'Kennedy Round', as the subsequent negotiations became known, was concerned with arranging 50 per cent tariff cuts only. The negotiations lasted for four years, and were several times on the verge of breaking down, and it was to the general surprise that agreement was finally reached in May 1967. The agreement was in fact almost entirely limited to the industrial products of developed countries. The US negotiators struggled to the end to include at least wheat, but France remained adamant, and the only significant agricultural provision was an agreement on providing an annual 5 million tons of food grains as aid to underdeveloped countries, of which the Six will contribute just under a quarter. A new definition of 'dumping' (normally understood as occurring when one country exports goods to another at less than their cost to produce and sell at home) was agreed to stop developed countries from putting up tariffs against goods from poor countries on this ground when the cheapness of the import in fact results from the low wages paid in the country of origin, but there was no success in reducing tariffs to zero on tropical products; neither Britain nor the EEC countries would abandon their preferences to some underdeveloped countries in order to meet the USA in this respect.

The substantial achievements of the Kennedy Round in progress towards freer trade between developed countries are nevertheless shown by the way in which protectionist opinion in the USA and elsewhere has since been rallying to try to undo the effect of this agreement. At present the tariffs on industrial products maintained by the CM, the USA and Britain average respectively 12, 17 and 18 per cent. In five years' time, when the Kennedy programme has been completed, it is estimated that average tariffs will range from 7 to 11 per cent. In these circumstances tariffs will cease to be a significant barrier to trade in industrial products between developed countries, whatever trading blocs may exist. The trade covered by these cuts is worth at present about £14,000 million a year; it is believed that the cuts will increase its value by about £1,100 million a year, or about 2 per cent of the value of world trade. However, when tariffs go it remains possible to block free trade by means of introducing direct physical controls on imports, and the protectionists' rearguard action may yet have some success in this respect.

THE UNDERDEVELOPED COUNTRIES AND WORLD TRADING ARRANGEMENTS

'The underdeveloped countries have rational grounds for asking the developed countries to liberalize their trade unilaterally. They need to be staunch free traders, and even preserve for themselves the right to give export subsidies, so far as the advanced countries' imports from them are concerned, but restrictionists in respect of their own imports. And they have valid arguments against anyone who would call this attitude logically inconsistent.'[1]

Certain economists began to put forward this sort of argument on behalf of the underdeveloped countries several years ago, but it is only recently that these countries have begun to organize themselves to make specific proposals and to take joint action in this direction. Having seen the changes which have taken place

[1] Gunnar Myrdal, *Economic Theory and Underdeveloped Regions*, Duckworth, 1957.

in world trading arrangements to the benefit of developed countries, they have begun to consider forms of reorganization to help themselves, in their far more desperate need to increase the value of their exports to pay for the imports necessary to development. At the UN Conference on Trade and Development of 1964, at which the underdeveloped countries appeared for the first time as a relatively unified pressure group, discussions centred on the calculation by the UN Secretariat on the further trade gap between the export earnings and the import requirements of the underdeveloped countries, on the basis of the growth target for the development decade of 5 per cent per annum. It was then estimated that this gap would be of the order of $20 billion by 1970, vastly exceeding any probable total of foreign aid; the figure has since tended to be revised downwards, but its actual value is of less importance than the concept, which emphasizes the need to concentrate on increasing the value of exports from the underdeveloped countries, as well as on increasing the flow of foreign aid to them.

The 1964 and subsequent UNCTAD meetings (it maintains a continuous secretariat) have been concerned with various proposals for changes in world trade organization and regulation, and specific requests for reform are due to be presented to the developed countries at the conference due in February 1968 at New Delhi. In the field of export promotion one set of proposals will be concerned with primary products, which at present account for about 80 per cent of underdeveloped countries' export earnings, and for which the underdeveloped countries would like to see new price raising or stabilizing agreements. Commodity agreements will be discussed in Chapter 13, but the possible concessions to be obtained from developed countries are considered—by the optimists—to consist broadly of their paying higher prices for those commodities only produced by underdeveloped countries, such as cocoa or coffee, and of their surrender of a larger share of world production to the underdeveloped countries of commodities like sugar or cotton which are produced by both, or for which the developed countries can produce artificial substitutes, such as rubber. Commodity agreements apart, exports of primary products could also be expanded if developed countries would agree to import them duty free and to refrain from imposing other controls or levying other taxes on them. The main remaining obstacles to removing tariffs from all primary products from underdeveloped countries are the preferential systems operated by Britain in favour of Commonwealth countries and the EEC in favour of its members' ex-overseas territories. The Latin American countries in particular, who benefit from no such preferences, would like to see both systems dismantled, and the USA has, as we have seen, agreed to abolish all its own tariffs on tropical agricultural products if the other developed countries will do the same. The possibility of agreement on the abolition of all such preferences in favour of general duty-free admission has consequently become one of UNCTAD's main pre-occupations, but even if the underdeveloped countries can agree on this among themselves, and the political obstacles to the abandonment of these links between developed and underdeveloped countries can be overcome, some developed countries, such as France, with strong traditions of protecting their own agriculture, will be unlikely to allow the unrestricted import of all foodstuffs from the underdeveloped countries. Some other countries, notably West Germany, also raise appreciable amounts of revenue from levying excise taxes on 'luxuries' like coffee and cocoa; an agreement to free the products of underdeveloped countries from such taxes would be a useful boost to their exports, but will be difficult to achieve, since its impact would differ greatly between developed countries.

Although primary products still account for so high a proportion of the underdeveloped countries' export earnings, some of the best prospects for the future lie in increasing export values by processing or semi-processing these products in their countries of origin. One of UNCTAD's most important aims is to get developed countries to abandon or at least reduce protection against manufactures from underdeveloped countries. In some cases such protection takes the form of direct controls—most countries impose quotas on imports of cotton textiles from Asian countries. Elsewhere protection is by means of tariffs, which the developed countries have been accustomed to argue are in any case low. UNCTAD discussions have drawn attention to the fact that the effective rate of protection on manufactures from under-developed countries is on the contrary normally high.[1]

Countries anxious to obtain reductions in barriers to their exports have, however, in normal international practice to offer concessions on their side. Underdeveloped countries are seldom in a position to do this; their shortage of foreign exchange earnings frequently obliges them to impose direct quantitative controls on imports, in order to make sure of being able to afford essentials, and their attempts to build up their own industries lead them to impose highly protective tariffs to enable these to make a start. Basically, therefore, they require the developed countries to liberalize trading rules in their favour without receiving any reciprocal advantage. To make bargaining more difficult still, they may need actually to increase their barriers against exports from the developed world.

TRADING ARRANGEMENTS BETWEEN
UNDERDEVELOPED COUNTRIES

In the past, the economic prescription favoured by most independent underdeveloped countries was to develop domestic industries as rapidly and as widely as possible in order to substitute domestic products for the imports which they could so ill afford. In a situation in which a large proportion of the labour force is otherwise unemployed, such a policy always makes a

[1] This is a phenomenon first pointed out by a Canadian economist, C. L. Barber. To give a modern example, the EEC has no tariff on imports of hides and skins, but a tariff of 16 per cent on leather products. This is an obvious obstacle to an underdeveloped country like India, trying to increase the value of exports, but the obstacle is much greater than at first appears. If we assume that the value of the skins increases by 50 per cent when they are turned into manufactured goods, the Indian producer of manufactures is at a disadvantage to the European producer in relation to this 50 per cent, and not in relation to the raw materials which they both get duty free. The 16 per cent tariff is therefore effectively 32 per cent and the European manufacturer benefits from a high rate of protection.

certain amount of economic sense. However, the policy of pressing forward with import substitution at all costs for markets often too small to support production at an efficient level, without the resources necessary to make use of modern technological advance, with shortages of managerial and other skills and under a degree of protection sufficient to prevent the competition which might encourage improvements in efficiency, has often led to very unimpressive results. There has consequently been a change in emphasis in development economics for these countries from what has been described as 'inward-looking industrialization' to policies of industrialization for export—which must be relatively efficient—and of industrialization to be carried out within groups of underdeveloped countries with the object of exporting to each other.

Since most underdeveloped countries have small populations, constituting in view of their low income per head even smaller markets for most modern manufacturing processes, the establishment of preferential trading blocs between them can lead to much more rational allocation of resources than if each tries to set up a full range of industries on its own account. The example of economic integration in Europe, with its threatening aspects to underdeveloped countries without special links with EEC countries or the UK, has encouraged imitation in the underdeveloped world. The Latin American Free Trade Area was established in 1960 and has now been joined by nine countries, including Mexico and the whole of the South American continent except for Bolivia, Venezuela and the Guianas. The participants have agreed to eliminate tariffs and other restrictions on their internal trade over a period of 12 years, with the additional aims of co-ordinating industrial and agricultural development policies. A treaty signed in the same year provided for the establishment of a customs union, within five years, between the five small countries of Central America, but this soon ran into disagreements over the speed of integration. There have been several proposals and agreements for closer trading links within Africa, nearly all either between franc area countries or sterling area countries, although one plan for a common market between Egypt, Ghana, Guinea, Mali and Morocco cut across the old colonial boundaries for a time. Very few of these proposals have in fact been implemented, and independent Africa now includes more tariff barriers than existed in colonial days. One recent achievement has, however, been the reconstitution of the East African Common Market, which had existed for 40 years but in which conflicting interests were threatening disintegration.

One of the main reasons for the slowness of the progress which has been made towards economic integration between under-developed countries is of course political; newly independent countries are normally highly nationalist in outlook and consequently find it difficult to surrender any degree of sovereignty under international agreements. Another common reason is a recurrent economic problem; underdeveloped countries vary considerably in degrees of poverty, and the establishment of an orthodox customs union or free trade area may very well work in favour of the richest members at the expense of the poorest. Industry is attracted to the richest area of the union because that is where the market is mainly concentrated and because it usually has the most highly developed infrastructure—the best power, water, transport and commercial services. The difference between the richest and poorest areas therefore becomes more and more pronounced; the poorest areas simply act as a market to the rest; they may even pay higher prices for their imports than they would have done if they had not instituted protection against the outside world, while they lose what savings they have since there are higher returns on investment elsewhere. This has been the experience of most economic unions where underdeveloped countries are concerned; the outstanding examples in recent years have been the East African Common Market, where the benefits have been largely concentrated in Kenya, and the now defunct Federation of Rhodesia and Nyasaland, round which a highly protective tariff enabled Southern Rhodesia to expand its exports to Northern Rhodesia and Nyasaland, which could previously buy more cheaply abroad. Such considerations mean that underdeveloped countries need to set up either much more sophisticated or much more limited international trade arrangements of this kind. If a customs union or a free trade area is established it requires built-in balancing provisions to protect the poorest members, as in the new East African Common Market, in which a member country with a trade deficit with another has the right to impose tariffs, for a limited time, on certain imports from the surplus country. Failing such provisions, which are undoubtedly complicated to work out and to operate, it is likely to be more generally advantageous for such countries to agree on free trade in certain commodities only, allocating a limited number of new industries between themselves for which they can together provide a large enough market by raising tariffs against the outside world.

Incidentally, international trading rules operate at present against just such arrangements. The basic principle of GATT is non-discrimination; members are not supposed to treat one trading partner more favourably than another. The exceptions are in the establishment of a customs union or free trade area, but these are required to be perfect examples of their kind; they must eliminate all tariffs on trade between members, on substantially all commodities. Such categorical requirements are obviously unsuited to the needs of underdeveloped countries. Although it now seems unlikely that in most cases any GATT members would invoke its rules to oppose the establishment of any such new trading arrangements among underdeveloped countries, they could usefully be reframed to give positive encouragement.

CHAPTER THIRTEEN

International Commodity Agreements

COMMODITY AGREEMENTS SINCE 1945

In the late 1940's commodity agreements were accepted as one of the forms of international action which could help to prevent the return of the economic disasters of the 1930's. The conception of such agreements which was embodied in the Havana Charter[1] of 1948 and in the General Agreement on Tariffs and Trade of 1947 was very different from that of the pre-war agreements, which had frequently been between producers alone, and were designed simply to extract the best possible price from consumers by means of restricting supply. It was now felt that these frankly monopolistic practices would not contribute to the expanding international economy which was the ideal inspiring the post-war monetary and trade agreements outlined in Chapter 9. The new commodity agreements, which were always to be between governments, must be accepted by consumers as well as producers, and each group would have an equal number of votes on the Commodity Councils which would govern the content and operation of the agreements. A procedure was laid down which involves the calling of a commodity study group by the United Nations to consider whether the conditions held to justify the establishment of an agreement exist. These conditions were defined as prevailing in the case of a 'burdensome surplus' or hardship for producers which will not respond to ordinary market forces. After the report of the study group, a full scale international conference follows. In the 20 years since this new approach was initiated, a mass of international groups and committees has been established.

[1] See Chapter 9, p. 104.

The two main aims of commodity agreements, according to the Havana Charter, were to moderate the large fluctuations in prices which were and are typical of many primary commodities, without interfering with long-term trends, and to promote any adjustments needed to put right the imbalance between production and consumption which is unfortunately still so common. It was not at this time one of the aims of commodity agreements to give the producers anything more than stability; over a number of years, the total of the producers' incomes would be the same with the agreement as without it. This is in sharp contrast with the present day ideology of commodity agreements, which is dealt with later in this chapter.

One of the most favoured techniques for the pursuit of the aims of the Havana Charter was the use of a 'buffer stock', under international management, which would be purchased when prices were low and sold when prices were high. Keynes, for instance, argued strongly that this instrument could both reduce short-term oscillations in prices and at the same time avoid isolating producers from long-term trends. A second technique, that of restricting exports, was less popular, and its use was subject under the Charter to specific conditions, designed to protect consumers and to avoid freezing the pattern of production.

The actual number and achievements of commodity agreements since the end of the 1940's have been modest, to say the least, and frequently the aims, method and scope of those there have been have not been on the lines envisaged in the Havana Charter. There have been four major formal agreements so far, covering wheat, tin, sugar and coffee. There is only room here to say enough about these to give some idea of the methods used and the problems encountered.

The International Wheat Agreement of 1949 was the first to come into force after the Second World War. It took three years and seven international conferences to arrive at this agreement, which in the end was not signed by two exporters, the USSR and Argentina. It was essentially a multilateral contract between exporters, who undertook to sell certain quantities at or below stated maximum prices, and importers, who undertook to buy certain quantities at or above stated minimum prices. Individual countries were free to negotiate deals with each other provided the prices were within the range laid down. The quantities covered by the agreement amounted to about two-thirds of world trade in wheat. It so happened that the first four-year agreement worked in favour of the importers, as the Korean war forced the free price above the agreement maximum, but it was nevertheless honoured by the exporters. There has been a long series of agreements since then, though at times the percentage of world trade covered has fallen to as little as 25 per cent and the basis of the undertakings has changed. Despite this the free price has remained within the agreement range from 1954 until very recently, and to that extent the agreements have been a success. However the experts' verdict is that the stabilization of prices has not been due to the agreements but to the national stocking policies of the USA and Canada, the two main exporters, which are both rich enough to carry stocks on a large scale. Moreover overproduction is currently becoming the problem, now that demand for imports from the communist countries and from India is falling away, and the agreement has no provisions to deal with this. It is therefore difficult to see the wheat agreements as an example of successful international action to solve problems which could not be solved by nations acting in isolation.

The International Sugar Agreement, which came into effect in 1954, had little in common with the Wheat Agreements, apart from including a price range accepted by both producers and consumers. The world's trade in sugar was already subject to certain special agreements, between the USA and its suppliers and between Britain and Commonwealth growers under the Commonwealth Sugar Agreements. The new international agreement applied to the residual 'free market', which represents only about 45 per cent of world trade, and is marked, partly for that reason, by violent fluctuations in price. Nearly all the countries buying on the free market, and most of the suppliers, including the USSR, were members. The instrument for keeping prices within the agreed range was to be adjustable export quotas. This technique involves agreeing 'basic quotas' for individual producing countries, usually based on an average of past exports, which are then adjusted upwards when prices exceed the maximum for a stated period, and downwards when prices fall below the minimum. The size of the adjustment was to be decided by the Sugar Council, but if agreement could not be reached it would be automatic—5 per cent in the case of a quota reduction and $7\frac{1}{2}$ per cent in the case of an increase. In addition, the exporters agreed to control production so that their carry-over stocks would not amount to more than 20 per cent of their basic quotas.

Sugar prices went above the maximum during and after the Suez crisis, but on the whole the agreement was sufficiently successful to be renewed from 1959 to 1961, with the addition of two more exporters. However, early in the new agreement prices fell below the minimum, despite the fact that quotas were reduced to 80 per cent of the basic tonnage, the lowest permitted by the agreement. Prices remained below the minimum for most of the second agreement, due to overproduction. This situation was made worse by the American decision in 1960 first to cut and then to ban imports from Cuba on political grounds. At a conference in the autumn of 1961 which met in an atmosphere of high stocks, low prices and Cuban demands for a hugely enlarged quota, it proved impossible to reach agreement on quotas for 1962. So ended the attempt to control the free market for sugar, and the result of this can be seen in the price index for the years since (1958 = 100):

1961	1962	1963	1964	1965	1966
77	79	237	163	58	50

After this experience it is not surprising that an attempt is being made to reach another international agreement.

The International Tin Agreement, which came into force in 1956 after intermittent negotiations stretching back to the establishment of a Study Group in 1947, was the only one to employ the favoured technique of the international buffer stock. The cost of the buffer stock is born by producers, who had to make compulsory contributions in three instalments (consumers did not take advantage of the provision for them to make voluntary contributions). Contributions could be either in tin or in cash, but as the cash equivalent of tin was fixed at the floor price of the range agreed between producers and consumers, contributions were naturally made in cash so long as the price remained above the minimum. The instructions to the manager of the buffer stock were related to the level of prices. When prices are in the middle third of the range, he can do nothing. When they are in the upper or lower third of the range he has discretion to sell or buy respectively. When the maximum price is reached he is obliged to sell—if necessary until the buffer stock is exhausted. Similarly when prices fall to the minimum, he is obliged to buy, if necessary until his cash is exhausted. Besides the buffer stock, provision was also made for the control of exports, but this is only permissible if there is a specified quantity of tin in the buffer stock.

The Tin Council has several times lost control of the market, even with the help of special contributions to the buffer stock, changes in the agreed range of prices, and heavy use of export restrictions during the first agreement. This has sometimes been due to special factors, such as the Suez crisis, which raised prices above the agreed maximum during the early days of the first agreement, and large sales by the USSR, which is not a member, which helped to depress prices in 1957–58. There were two years of relative stability in 1959 and 1960, but for much of the period of the second and third agreements, from mid-1961 onwards, prices have been well above the current agreement maximum because production has been running behind demand despite large sales from the US stockpile. Consequently the price range has been raised many times; in the periods when the current price range corresponds to the market situation the operations of the buffer stock still exert a modest stabilizing effect.

The 1962 International Coffee Agreement is not only the most recent of the four commodity agreements which have come into force since the war, but also represents the greatest departure from the ideas of the Havana Charter and is for that reason in many ways a model for the agreements which many underdeveloped countries would like to conclude for other commodities. This is so despite the fact that the normal United Nations procedure was followed of study group and conference with full representation of consumers. The agreement was reached at a time when world stocks, chiefly in Brazil and Colombia, were equal to about 18 months' worth of world exports. An expert report proposed an agreement embodying a controlled reduction

in prices, the internationalization of stocks, and other sophisticated devices. This was rejected in favour of a simple export
restriction scheme with the explicit aim of 'assuring that the
general level of coffee prices does not decline below the general
level of such prices in 1962'. It is true the agreement does refer to
the producers' obligation to restrain production, and to the aim of
establishing a collective policy on stocks, but the wording is so
loose and action since 1962 has been so meagre that this does not
amount to much more than piety. An FAO publication of 1967
comments 'No agreement has been obtained on individual production goals under the Agreement, but FAO, IBRD and the
International Coffee Organization are continuing their joint
study. . . . The proposal of the Executive Director of the International Coffee Organization is to bring current supply and
demand into balance by reducing world production . . . by
1971/72.'[1] It seems clear that the agreement secures for the
producers a price that is well above the equilibrium level at which
supply and demand would be equal in an average year, and yet
does not so far implement any measures to restrict production.
This is a far cry from the Havana Charter with its heartfelt
reference to 'the desirability of securing long-term equilibrium
between the forces of supply and demand'.

The Coffee Agreement has been successful in its price objectives; from 1963 to 1966 prices were not only maintained but
were higher than the 1962 levels. The techniques used were
refined by the introduction of agreed price ranges for four main
types of coffee, to make possible selective adjustments of quotas
for the four corresponding groups of exporting countries. But
the agreement is under severe strain, partly because its very
success in lifting prices stimulates overproduction. A symptom of
this is the rapid growth in exports nominally directed to 'new
markets', to which quotas do not apply; nearly two-thirds of all
new market exports in the 1965/66 quota year was probably
'tourist coffee', coffee which was in fact diverted, with enormous
profits for the middlemen, to quota markets. The ICO is trying
to prevent this by encouraging the consuming countries to take
stricter policing action on imports, but to the extent that it is

[1] *FAO Commodity Review, 1967.*

successful it will increase the strains on the agreement. The current negotiation of a new agreement, which involves the question of future quotas, is proving extremely arduous.

The position of the consuming countries in the Coffee Agreement is hardly what the framers of the post-war commodity policies would have expected. They have not only agreed to pay what are in effect monopoly prices, but they have actually forced the agreement upon some exporters who would have preferred not to join. These include the low cost, high quality producers of East Africa, who could sell more coffee at lower prices, but are obliged to join the agreement since otherwise their largest markets would be closed to them. This peculiar outcome is caused by the same mixture of altruism and politics which is the source of foreign aid. The USA announced its support for a coffee agreement soon after the inauguration of the 1961 Alliance for Progress; President Kennedy pointed out that a fall of one cent in the price of a pound of green coffee cost Latin American producers about 50 million dollars a year, 'enough seriously to undercut what we are seeking to accomplish by the Alliance'.[1] It was undoubtedly this political concern, particularly focused on Brazil, which led to the establishment of the agreement.

There are two other agreements which will shortly or probably be coming into force. The first is an informal export restriction scheme for hard fibres (chiefly sisal and henequen). This came into effect in 1968. Basic quotas are being allocated to the exporting countries on the usual basis of an average of past exports, and these will be cut by 4·8 per cent. The market is suffering from a surplus caused by high planting in the boom price years of 1963 and 1964, and partly by the erosion of demand in certain end uses as a result of competition from synthetics. In this situation the scope for a price increase advantageous to producers was small. It was significant that the producers proposed a target minimum price £10 per ton higher than the price ruling at the time of the meeting, which was the lowest since the war, whereas the consumers argued that it should be no more than £5 higher. It remains to be seen how this agreement works out.

[1] Quoted in *The World's Coffee*, J. W. F. Rowe, London, HMSO, 1963.

The second new agreement, which has been planned in detail but not yet ratified, is for cocoa. As so often, negotiations have stretched out over many years. In this case the consumers seem to have persisted in protecting their own interests, and this explains why, to judge from press reports, the result seems to return to the Havana Charter principles. There have been attacks by merchants in the UK and the USA on the narrowness and artificially high level of the price range, which will be supported by quotas and a buffer stock. But in fact the top of the range is 45 per cent above the bottom, while prices have been below the minimum only in three of the last seventeen years but above the maximum in eight of them. Quotas do not come into force unless prices are at or below the mid-point of the range. The buffer stock, which will be financed by a levy on exports, will buy the excess production when quotas are in force. The important point is that the buffer stock buying price will usually be half the minimum price, and when the buffer stock purchases reach their maximum the price will fall to less than one fifth of the minimum price. Provided that producers do not yield to the temptation to exceed their quotas, these prices will be some disincentive to overproduction.

Apart from the agreements proper described above, some valuable though less far-reaching results have been achieved by several of the many study groups set up under the post-war procedures. These have, for example, improved statistics and led to various degrees of co-operation short of agreements but sometimes including production cuts or promotion efforts.

THE VALUE OF COMMODITY AGREEMENTS

The proportion of world trade in primary commodities covered by the international agreements which have been described is in total small. The large item of petroleum is not covered at all, though this hardly matters since world demand grows so fast. Tin is the only non-ferrous metal covered, while of agricultural commodities perhaps about one third of world trade by value is covered if the Commonwealth and US Sugar Agreements are included and the new hard fibre and cocoa agreements are given the benefit of the doubt. Nearly half of the trade covered is moreover in wheat and flour, whose main exporters are developed countries.

How far is it likely or desirable that the coverage of commodity agreements will or should be extended in future? Obviously there are enormous difficulties in reaching and operating these agreements. The length and frequent failure of negotiations, the complexity of the agreement documents, and the failures to attain their objectives all demonstrate this. The main sources of these difficulties may be summarized as the divergence of interests between producers and consumers, the diversity of interests among producers, and the frequent unpredictable changes in the economic and political factors affecting particular commodities. And yet a few agreements have been reached and have achieved their aims, however modest and however precariously. On the whole, although difficulties can be foreseen in almost every case, some increase in the coverage of agreements can be expected.

The economic desirability of commodity agreements is a highly controversial subject. For purposes of discussion it is helpful to distinguish the two aims of increasing and of stabilizing the export receipts of primary producing countries, though they are often difficult to separate in practice. Violent fluctuations in export prices can cause distress and waste of resources (and may make the commodity concerned less attractive to consumers in the long run as well). They can seriously hold back the development of a country that is heavily dependent on one or two crops, and lacks large reserves of foreign currency, by reducing its capacity to import investment goods or to borrow. Some economists take this argument very seriously and believe that commodity agreements are justified if they have a moderating effect on fluctuations in export earnings caused by price changes, and it is true that, despite all difficulties, a few agreements which offer little more than stabilization have been made and operate successfully.

On the other hand, the opposing school argues that pure stabilization by itself is not really attractive to most producers, and that this is proved by the small number of successful international agreements and of individual countries which have adopted national policies to encourage stabilization.[1] Recent

[1] 'Stabilization of Proceeds from Raw Material Exports.' H. C. Wallich

research has suggested that the difference between developed and underdeveloped countries as far as instability of exports is concerned is much smaller than is often assumed, and a new study of twelve underdeveloped countries has also failed to discover more than a weak relationship between investment and the purchasing powers of exports.[1] More investigation of these relationships is required to discover just how valuable stabilization would really be, but some support is provided for the view that fluctuations may be less important than is usually supposed by the low demand so far shown by underdeveloped countries for the credit facility established by the IMF in 1963 to compensate member countries for temporary cuts in export earnings. By May 1967 only eight countries had made use of this, to a total value of about $180 million. However, the rules governing this facility have now been liberalized, and its value in a peak year could now be as high as $1,300 million, and it remains to be seen what new use will be made of it. Credit of this kind has of course to be repaid, but its effect should be very similar to those of pure stabilization. On the whole, these arguments and this evidence suggest that the countries involved may have been right in thinking that only in special cases is the trouble of full-blown commodity agreements worthwhile.

The question of increasing, as opposed to stabilizing, the export earnings or prices of primary producing countries, is quite separate. Developed countries supply nearly half the world's exports of primary commodities, but the argument for increasing earnings is of course usually put with the underdeveloped countries in mind. One important way of achieving this, which most economists would endorse, would be to reduce the protection and subsidization given by many industrialized countries to their agricultural production, either for internal consumption or for export. Other measures would be for rich countries to reduce revenue duties on imports from underdeveloped countries and to remove protection for their own processing industries (see in *Economic Development for Latin America*, H. S. Ellis, ed. New York, 1961.

[1] Alisdair I. Macbean, *Export Instability and Economic Development*, Allen and Unwin, 1967.

Chapter 12, pp. 155–7). The underdeveloped countries are pushing these demands in UNCTAD and elsewhere, often in association with proposals for new commodity agreements. However
these demands are essentially for fair competition, and this does
not necessarily need to be embodied in a commodity agreement.

Two other ideas are commonly discussed, which are really
about restrictions on trade in favour of underdeveloped countries.
One, which seems most unlikely to be implemented, is that
developed countries should restrict research into synthetics and
their uses where this is likely to lead to a reduction in demand for
a 'natural' commodity. The other is for the formation of cartels
of underdeveloped countries to force up the price of their exports
by restricting supplies—a plan which of course depends on the
absence of synthetic substitutes. The experience of the International Coffee Agreement has shown the second of these ideas
to be feasible provided the political and economic pattern
is favourable. Economists' views about the desirability of such
agreements again differ sharply. According to one who believes
that pure stabilization is the proper function of international
commodity agreements, 'The use of commodity control schemes
deliberately to ensure artificially high prices is a throwback to the
interwar period . . . the negation of the Havana Charter-United
Nations conception . . . it amounts to the prostitution of control
schemes. . . .'[1] These strong feelings are based on the theoretical
view that if prices do not reflect costs, the result is bound to be a
misallocation of resources which will make the world as a whole
poorer than it would otherwise be. Other economists maintain
that stabilization alone is small beer and that producers' cartels
are the best way of improving the terms of world trade in favour
of the underdeveloped countries.

Arguments about what measures are most likely to maximize
the wealth of the world as a whole will certainly not be settled by
appealing to factual evidence, and although disguised as economic
theory may be best regarded as expressions of political points of

[1] J. W. F. Rowe, *Primary Commodities in International Trade*, p. 216.
Cambridge 1965, on which this chapter draws heavily, as on Gerda
Blau's *International Commodity Arrangements and Policies*, FAO, Rome,
1964.

view. It is more useful here to mention two dangers which both sides would agree to be inherent in international agreements to restrict supplies. One is the accumulation of surplus production; it has for example been estimated that if present policies are not changed there will be nearly two years' supply of coffee in stock by 1970. The second is that the quotas settled at the beginning of an agreement tend to freeze the pattern of production between countries, irrespective of changes in relative costs. These two points are of course linked, since it is the maintenance of high prices which tends to prevent relatively high cost production from becoming unprofitable and disappearing in favour of new low cost capacity.

It has been suggested that both these dangers could be avoided by means of a variable export duty or levy. The obligation to impose or increase such a duty, if stocks in a producing country reached a specified level in relation to its quota, would become a condition of retaining a quota under the agreement. A second new provision would be that in the periodical redistribution of quotas preference would be given to the lowest cost producers. The size of the export levy needed to match a particular country's production with its quota would be evidence of its costs—the higher the levy, the lower cost production would tend to be. Countries where the export levy was higher than average would get their basic quotas increased and vice versa. Needless to say there would be innumerable practical problems, particularly of definition. Economic decisions on production and prices are moreover so politically potentially explosive that it is hard to imagine all the parties to an international agreement accepting arrangements with so large an automatic element in their operation. Nevertheless these suggestions undoubtedly make economic sense, and much progress would have been made if producing countries could at least be brought to acknowledge that the gains from an export restriction scheme should not all be passed on to the producers and that schemes should have scope for the reallocation of quotas on the basis of costs.

Even if the problems of overproduction and the pattern of output could be solved, however, there would still be limits to the usefulness of agreements designed to raise prices. It must be remembered that it is only in the case of a few commodities—mainly coffee, cocoa, tea and bananas, which account for only about one-fifth of total primary commodity trade—that poor countries do in fact have an effective monopoly of production. For most others there is competition from domestic production in importing countries, from the exports of rich temperate countries, or from synthetics or other close substitutes. Of the under-developed countries' monopolies, coffee is by far the biggest, and as a coffee agreement already exists there is little prospect of further price raising agreements making a really significant contribution to the development of the poor countries as a whole, although the impact on individual countries might be considerable.

A final point about price-raising agreements is that their justification is that they are an addition to other forms of foreign aid, and one that does not involve poor countries in assuming any burden of repayment or interest charges. At the present time, when conventional sources of aid seem to be dwindling, this is of course a very strong point in their favour. Yet it must be faced that to distribute aid in proportion to the production by particular countries of particular commodities is a hit or miss method which is not necessarily either equitable or efficient, since it takes no account of income per head, balance of payments situations or the 'absorptive capacity' of recipient countries. This is of course true of other forms of aid distributed for historical or political reasons, but it means that there is nothing specially desirable about com-modity agreements as a form of aid, if some other international mechanism for diverting a similar amount of money is available.

This chapter has stressed the difficulties and disadvantages of commodity agreements in order to explain the modest scale of the achievement in this field so far, and to make it clear that they are by no means a panacea, whether the aim is the pure stabilization of prices or pushing prices up above the free market level and hence effecting a transfer of income from rich to poor countries. However, given an imperfect world without supra-national co-ordination and with no adequate aid-giving mechanism, the agree-ments which have been made are a remarkable example of human ingenuity and co-operation. Those that exist are valuable, and it is likely that there will be some increase in their use in future.

CHAPTER FOURTEEN

International Monetary Reform

THE ESTABLISHMENT OF THE IMF

The post-war establishment of the International Monetary Fund was as we have seen the first attempt to deal with world[1] monetary problems by means of an international controlling organization.[2] From the time of the emergence of modern industrial economies, world trade had been carried out under two international monetary systems, and had suffered under the disintegration of both. The first, the gold standard, which operated up to the First World War, was a truly international system. All important trading countries held their reserves almost entirely in the form of gold; their currencies were defined in terms of gold at a fixed rate—and hence were fixed in relation to each other—and were freely convertible into gold, which was freely imported and exported. The normal unit of international transactions was the pound sterling, and the efficiency of the system was increased by the fact that London acted as a single great clearing centre for nearly all international payments. London bankers were not in control of the system, although contributing to its smooth working; it was in fact an automatic operation, not amenable to either national or international control. As long as a country was on the gold standard, a balance of payments deficit was inevitably followed by a loss of reserves; money became scarce, deflation and rising unemployment followed and the downwards spiral continued until the scarcity of money forced interest rates up to a level at which gold began to flow back into the country. The reverse process occurred in a country with a balance of payments surplus, and there was little the government concerned could do to change the situation in either case.

[1] In this chapter 'world' is the non-communist world.
[2] See Chapter 9.

174

After the disruptions caused by the First World War, most countries were anxious to return to the gold standard as soon as they could stabilize prices and build up sufficient reserves for this to be practicable. There was however a world shortage of gold, production having declined sharply from its pre-war levels and failing to recover for several years. The international monetary system which was reconstructed during the 1920's, when most countries managed to fix their currencies once more to gold, differed for this reason from the old gold standard in that countries now began to hold their reserves not only in the form of gold but also in the form of internationally acceptable currencies, the 'reserve' currencies of the British pound and the American dollar. This much more complicated 'gold exchange' system gave rise to new problems. The level of world liquidity—i.e. the total of world reserves, or the stock of internationally acceptable means of payment—no longer depended simply on gold; it could actually be reduced if a reserve currency began to be converted into gold, as it might be as a result of a lack of faith in the economic progress of the country concerned. At the same time the need for liquidity increased with the arrival of speculation in the future of the three units of payment in relation to each other. This arose because the gold exchange standard was no longer a system of fixed exchange rates; governments were no longer content to accept the automatic operation of an international monetary system, but were beginning to operate national monetary policies with the object of controlling the balance of payments rather than of being controlled by it. Nearly all countries now established national central banks, which tried to influence the level of reserves by changes in the exchange rate, or to maintain artificially stable exchange rates by means of controls on the flow of money out of the country. Whereas the old system was plainly unsatisfactory because it prevented national action to check deflation, the new system was equally unsatisfactory in its international aspects; national monetary policies could not be successful without international co-operation. In the fiasco of the 1930's devaluation of its currency by one country would lead to a round of competitive depreciations after which nobody's position was improved and everyone's confidence was further undermined, and the proliferation of exchange controls produced an increasing number of direct barriers to international trade.

In the new atmosphere of international co-operation which existed after the Second World War, therefore, world monetary reform was a high priority for a programme of international reorganization. The obvious pitfalls of both the old systems were clear; it was agreed that governments must, as they could not under the old gold standard, be able to operate their own monetary policies with the object of controlling the level of domestic economic activity, but that at the same time such policies had to be contained within an international system which would ensure normally stable exchange rates, avoid the need to impose exchange controls, and would hence establish a free flow of international trade. Beyond these basic assumptions, however, monetary experts differed. It was felt that countries faced with balance of payments deficits should have some access to an international stock of reserves to enable them to solve at least temporary problems without resorting to the deflationary policies which would affect their trading partners as well as themselves, and it was also realized that such a stabilizing mechanism could usefully work the other way, to discourage countries from continuing to build up reserves by maintaining a balance of payments surplus and so causing shortages for others. But there was considerable disagreement on the suitable extent of international assistance on the one hand and international restrictions on the other, and there was also wide divergence of opinion on the question of whether the total level of world liquidity should be the subject of radical reform or minor adjustment.

The most comprehensive plan for international monetary reform put forward at the time was Keynes' plan for an International Clearing Union, and its scope shows the limitations of the compromise which was eventually reached in the establishment of the IMF. Keynes' proposal was in effect for a world central bank, which would hold deposits in terms of a new international currency unit, which he called Bancor, which would be fixed (though not unalterably) in terms of gold. The depositors would be the national central banks of the member countries, who would not be allowed to hold foreign currencies as part of their reserves, which would only consist of gold and bancor. Depositors would only be allowed to use their balances to make transfers to the accounts of other members, so that the system as a whole would necessarily be in balance. A country in balance of payments deficit would be able to use overdraft facilities, up to a quota fixed in relation to the value of its foreign trade, on which interest charges would be paid. A country with a large balance of payments surplus would be encouraged to increase its imports or to make loans to other countries by means of interest charges, which the Clearing Union would levy on any credit balances in excess of half the member's quota. In Keynes' view, the level of world liquidity needed to be determined by the international monetary authority, and not 'in an unpredictable and irrelevant manner, as, for example, by the technical progress of the gold industry, nor subject to large variations depending on the gold reserve policies of individual countries; but . . . governed by the actual current requirements of world commerce, and . . . capable of deliberate expansion and contraction to offset deflationary and inflationary tendencies in effective world demand.'[1] In the International Clearing Union, world liquidity would have expanded whenever a central bank needed to draw on its overdraft facilities, thus creating new bancor deposits for other central banks, and have been reduced whenever a debtor paid off its overdraft. The potential level of world liquidity would also continue to increase as members' quotas rose with increases in their foreign trade.

The surrender of national sovereignty involved in such a scheme was, however, too great for it to be accepted. The agreement which was finally reached in the establishment of the IMF was not a radical reform, but a structure added on to the existing gold exchange system which, it was hoped, would improve its operation. The quotas which members subscribe to the IMF were fixed on a very much smaller scale than was envisaged for a world central bank; each quota was determined according to such considerations as the size of the member's national income, foreign trade and reserves, and they totalled at first $7·9 billion, or about 7 per cent

[1] *Proposals for an International Clearing Union*, Cmd 6437, HMSO, 1943.

of the value of world trade in that year (1949). Keynes had tentatively suggested quotas at a level of 75 per cent of the value of each member's foreign trade, averaged over the last three to five years. It was agreed that IMF quotas should be paid 25 per cent in gold and 75 per cent in the member's own currency, each member being allowed to purchase any foreign currency required from the Fund in exchange for its own currency, until IMF holdings of its own currency reach 200 per cent of its quota. By this means world reserves are in a sense increased on a modest scale, since currencies go into circulation which would otherwise have remained unused in the account of the creditor country, and countries with temporary balance of payments deficits are provided with a limited credit which may enable them to solve their problems without resorting to deflation. The question of discouraging countries from maintaining balance of payments surpluses to the inconvenience of their trading partners, a possibility which appeared at the time of the Bretton Woods meeting to apply only to the USA, was partly met by a clause enabling the IMF to declare that a currency has become 'scarce' (i.e. within the Fund as a whole and not only for some of its members), in which case members become free to impose exchange controls on that currency. Otherwise members agreed to eliminate all exchange controls as soon as possible. They also agreed to promote exchange stability by submitting any proposed change in the value of their currencies (if in excess of 10 per cent) to the IMF for approval; Fund permission is given only if its directors are satisfied that the change is necessary to correct a 'fundamental disequilibrium', but national independence is safeguarded by the provision that objections should not be made 'because of the domestic social or political policies of the member proposing the change'.

THE OPERATION OF THE IMF AND WORLD MONETARY PROBLEMS

Owing to the small scale on which it had been founded, the IMF was in fact unable to play an important part in world monetary

TABLE 8

World Reserves (held by National Monetary Authorities) and IMF Positions

($ billion)

End of year	Gold	US$	UK£	Total foreign exchange*	IMF gold tranche	IMF credit tranche	Total plus IMF credit
1949	33·2	3·1	7·9	10·5	1·7	6·2	51·5
1953	34·4	6·0	8·1	17·2	1·9	7·1	60·6
1957	37·3	8·3	7·2	19·0	2·3	7·2	65·8
1961	38·9	11·1	7·6	22·4	4·2	12·8	78·2
1965	41·4	14·2	6·7	22·6	5·4	12·4	81·7

World reserves as a percentage of world imports:

1953 74; 1957 57; 1961 54; 1965 43.

Source: IMF.

* Including others.

affairs for the first ten years or so of its existence. Europe's enormous requirements for foreign exchange were met by a flow of dollars directly from the USA in the form of grants and loans, later supplemented by payments agreements between the European countries. For the first decade after the war, the working of the gold exchange system was made possible by this dollar flow; world gold stocks increased very gradually, and sterling reserves were no larger in 1956 than in 1949, so that the increase in world liquidity was nearly all due to the greater use of the dollar as a reserve currency. World reserves held in dollars were less than a tenth the value of reserves held in gold, and less than half of reserves held in sterling, in the late 1940's; by 1956 the proportion of dollars to gold had risen to nearly a quarter, and dollar reserves were bigger than sterling reserves. Countries were working towards the abolition of exchange controls, but under US encouragement and through intra-European agreements rather than under the auspices of the IMF. International authority received an initial setback in 1948, when France ignored the Fund's refusal of permission for a discriminatory form of devaluation, although a year later it conformed once more to IMF rules. The 1949 round of devaluations took place with IMF approval, although their consequences later came to be considered too harsh, and devaluation tended to go out of fashion as an instrument of economic policy. The post-war monetary system has in fact become far more rigid than the Bretton Woods planners envisaged; in contrast to the excessive instability of the pre-war years, there is now excessive resistance to changing exchange rates in either direction.

Although the international instrument of control was by-passed for several years after the war, there was nevertheless an unprecedented degree of international co-operation in monetary affairs. US assistance to Europe was reciprocated in the late 1950's, when the American balance of payments deficit became a problem. A series of bilateral agreements were made between the USA and various European countries to help finance this without the loss of too much gold from the US reserves, and an increasing degree of co-operation between European central banks followed, largely to help the UK with its similar difficulties. Other international bodies were established for the purpose of regular consultation on monetary affairs—a monetary committee within OECD, the managing board of the European Monetary Agreement, the informal 'Basle group' of central bankers, and latterly the monetary committee of the EEC. Meanwhile the IMF gradually began to play a more active role. At the time of the Suez crisis in 1956 both France and Britain drew on their IMF quotas, and in 1958 it was agreed to increase quotas by 50 per cent. The Fund enlarged its own usefulness by developing a technique of 'standby' credits, by which a member country in difficulties can have a credit officially arranged for it, but does not need to make the actual drawing if the arrangement itself proves sufficient to support its currency against speculation. It was further strengthened in 1961/62 by the 'General Arrangements to Borrow'. These ensured a much more adequate supply of the main currencies without altering quotas (and hence voting strengths in the Fund). The ten main industrial countries agreed to lend their own currencies, up to stated limits, directly to the Fund in time of need, although the final decision as to how much credit to make available lies in this case with the ten countries and not with the IMF.

Early in the 1960's, a new concern began to be felt about the working of the international monetary system, which led to a revival of interest in genuinely international means of control. The main reason for this change of atmosphere was the realization that the US balance of payments deficit was likely to continue for some years, while the other reserve currency country, the UK, was also faced with recurrent balance of payments difficulties. This underlined the weakness of the gold exchange system; further additions to world reserves depend mainly on an increasing flow of dollars and sterling from the reserve currency countries, and attempts by these to cure their balance of payments problems thus work directly against an increase in world liquidity. On the other hand, failure to cure such problems leads to speculation against the currency concerned; world liquidity can be reduced by the conversion of a reserve currency into gold, and since neither currency is backed by sufficient gold to meet the demands of those liquidating their holdings, a major loss of confidence in either currency might result, it was argued, in the collapse of the system as a whole. This prospect seemed distant, if highly alarming. A more immediate problem, at least in the opinion of some authorities, was that of the future supply of world liquidity. Monetary experts differ sharply on the subject of whether there is sufficient liquidity at present to enable world trade to flow as smoothly as possible. Those who believe that it is already inadequate argue that modern liquidity requirements are much larger, in relation to the volume of world trade, than was the case before the war, since governments are no longer so willing to try to cure their balance of payments problems by means of deflation, and have agreed not to use direct import controls. They must therefore finance deficits for longer periods from their own reserves or by borrowing. Reserves also need to be larger because of the increased amounts of speculation between the three units of international settlement. Since the ratio of world reserves to world imports has been falling in recent years (from over 80 per cent in 1950 to 43 per cent in 1965; see Table 8), this school of thought maintains that the problem is already serious. Their opponents argue that the post-war levels of world reserves were in fact excessive, and point out that the proportion under the old gold standard was as little as 20 per cent. However, it is generally agreed that whatever the present situation may be, there is clearly a problem for the future, since both the USA and the UK must attempt to cure their balance of payments problems. There can be no further substantial increase in the supply of either of the existing reserve currencies, while world gold holdings have been rising in recent years by little more than one per cent per annum, and have small prospect of increasing faster than this.

Another major defect of the present system which has become apparent since it has been realized that most governments now agree on the undesirability of changes in exchange rates, is known as the 'adjustment' problem. An international monetary system should have a built-in mechanism of adjustment to long-term changes in international costs and prices. Under the old gold standard, such changes led to deflation or inflation in the country concerned, until prices conformed once more to world levels; between the wars, governments were more than ready to revalue their currencies in line with such changes, at least in a downwards direction if costs were rising, in order to cheapen their exports and reduce imports. Modern governments have as their main economic objectives the maintenance of high levels of employment and growth (though in some cases, notably France and Germany, the avoidance of inflation tends to have an even higher priority). For these reasons governments tend to be very reluctant to revalue their currencies or to allow more than a modest degree of deflation, and a long-term change in international costs tends to result in a long-term balance of payments deficit or surplus. While the present international monetary system has some resources from which to assist countries with temporary balance of payments deficits, it has proved to have very little means of influencing countries in surplus to restore the balance, and can offer no long-term solutions to either trend.

Finally, as with the other post-war measures to increase international co-operation, the problems of the underdeveloped countries were given little weight in the establishment of the IMF. Underdeveloped countries, as primary producers, have violent seasonal and annual fluctuations in their international payments. They are nearly all short of reserves to meet these fluctuations, and with the decline in commodity prices of recent years reserves have become shorter still. As a result these countries are obliged to cut imports essential for development and to impose complex import and exchange controls. Since their need for capital for investment is so great, they are not in a position to build up reserves from their own resources. The international monetary system evolved in the post-war years offered no solution to these countries' payments problems.

PROPOSALS FOR FURTHER REFORMS OF THE INTERNATIONAL MONETARY SYSTEM

The realization of the existence of these major defects in the modern gold exchange system—the problems of confidence, of adjustment, of long-term liquidity requirements and of the underdeveloped countries—led in the early 1960's to a new interest in proposals for its reform. Such proposals have ranged from suggestions for various changes to improve the working of the present system to plans for its radical alteration. Their discussion has tended to show a division of opinion between monetary experts in the reserve currency countries and those in the other leading industrial economies, although this shows signs of being reduced as the problems of managing a reserve currency have begun to seem greater and greater. Traditionally, the leading industrial countries whose currencies are not normally used as world reserves, in particular France and West Germany, have tended to resent the potential profits and world economic influence accruing to the reserve currency countries, and they have consequently tended to put forward proposals designed to reduce the roles of the pound and the dollar. Recently, however, Britain and the USA have also begun to see advantages in divesting themselves of this responsibility; the profits to their banking and financial sectors and the opportunities for the use of foreign capital which it involves are now tending to be outweighed, especially for the UK, by the limitations which are imposed on domestic economic policy through the constant need to maintain confidence in the reserve currency and hence to avoid balance of payments deficits. As a result, international views on monetary reform have grown closer together.

The necessity for change began to be discussed officially in 1962, when the ten leading developed countries set up a Study Group to review the functioning of the international monetary system. The Group concluded that the present system of fixed exchange rates based on the present price of gold was still basically acceptable. They were not concerned by the confidence problem, and indeed the way in which the USA and several European countries rallied to assist the UK in the sterling crisis which developed in the following year gave considerable justification to this opinion. They proposed 'further study' for the adjustment problem, but on the liquidity question suggested that there was an immediate need for a moderate increase in IMF quotas, and admitted that there might be a possible future need for a new kind of international reserve asset. This had already been proposed under various forms, the simplest being an agreement to use some of the other strong currencies, such as the West German mark and the French and Swiss francs, as additional key currencies. The US government had in fact declared that in the event of its achieving a balance of payments surplus it would avoid lowering the level of world reserves by reducing dollar liabilities held abroad, but would instead acquire foreign currencies to hold in its own reserves. A gold exchange system with several key currencies would of course have the disadvantage of offering a wide scope for speculation between them, with consequent sudden flows of capital in and out of the countries concerned. Various schemes to reduce this disadvantage, such as undertakings by the key currency countries to hold reserves in certain fixed proportions of gold and currencies, or to pay off deficits in similar fixed proportions, have also been put forward.

One government, the French, began however at this point to support a suggestion for a radical change in the system. The French monetary expert Jacques Rueff has been one of the main proponents of a return to the old gold standard, an idea which has found sympathy with General de Gaulle. Rueff has argued that the present gold exchange standard is in permanent danger of collapse, since fears of devaluation by either the US or the UK lead to periodic flights from these currencies and to the hoarding of gold, a policy which France in fact began to follow officially in 1965, demanding gold from the USA in exchange for dollar liabilities and accumulating as a result an eighth of the world's gold reserves (1967). In the French view, based on bitter past experience, inflation is a far worse threat than unemployment, and they believe that the workings of the gold exchange standard have caused inflation to be spread abroad from the reserve currency countries. With a return to the old gold standard, a country losing gold would naturally have its money supply reduced and (in Rueff's view) would then reduce prices and wages to cheapen exports. (In practice of course the result would not be lower wages but unemployment.) Rueff would achieve a return to the gold standard by means of doubling the world price of gold. Since gold still constitutes more than half of world reserves (see Table 8), this would mean that world reserves even with the abandonment of the reserve currencies would be substantially increased.

The world liquidity problem as a whole would be solved, and annual gold production would increase (the price of gold has been fixed at $35 an ounce since 1934, and many mines are uneconomic at that level). The reserve problems of individual countries would not of course be equally improved, since the increase would go to the gold hoarders and benefit the countries which have tried to co-operate in working the gold exchange system much less. This is only one of the reasons why other countries are never likely to agree to this plan. A return to an automatically operating system which would so much reduce the scope of government action to control the level of economic activity would generally be considered a regressive step, while another consideration is that major benefits would accrue to the two main gold producers, the USSR and South Africa, which are not two of the most popular governments in the international community.

Several other plans have been put forward for radical changes in the international monetary system, but none have been given significant government support. Many economists have pointed out that theoretically both the liquidity and adjustment problems would cease to exist if currencies were no longer fixed in relation to gold, but exchange rates were allowed to move freely—even from day to day—in relation to supply and demand. In practice the uncertainties which such a system would present to international trade and capital movements are felt to be too great to be tolerated, and all the governments of the main trading countries are firmly committed to a fixed exchange rate system. Other experts have drawn up new proposals for an international central bank operating an international credit currency which would eventually dispense with the need for gold. These have been variations on Keynes' original plan; one of the best known is that of Professor Triffin, under which countries would deposit their reserves with an expanded IMF, which would have the power to increase or reduce world liquidity as it saw fit by buying or selling securities in the open market. Another plan, proposed by Maxwell Stamp, would not give the IMF the role of a full world central bank, but would give it the power to create new world reserves with the object of simultaneously solving the problems of world liquidity and of the underdeveloped countries. The IMF would issue certificates, to be accepted as international currency, to a certain value (the initial amount suggested was $3 billion), for distribution to the governments of the underdeveloped countries. These countries would use them to pay for imports, so that the amount issued would gradually be added to the reserves of the developed world.

A number of other proposals have been made to deal with the payments problems of poor countries dependent on exports of commodities with widely fluctuating values, mainly to the effect that the rich countries importing from them, who profit from their price falls, should make funds available to be used as credits by underdeveloped countries at times when export values fall below average, to be repaid when they rise above average. Special drawing rights on the IMF have now in fact been arranged for underdeveloped countries faced with an unexpected cut in export earnings due to a sudden price fall, and the UNCTAD meeting due in 1968 is expected to discuss an enlargement of this scheme.

CHANGES IN 1967/68—THE GOLD CRISIS

In 1966 world reserves, which had normally been rising by about 7 per cent a year, showed no increase. The leading members of the IMF consequently agreed that despite their differences of opinion as to the method of reforming the international monetary system, the time had come to make some further provisions for additions to world liquidity. The French still wanted to increase the price of gold, the Americans and British to create some form of new reserve unit to supplement the existing three, and the British government now made it plain that it was in fact willing to withdraw sterling from its role as a reserve currency if a means of achieving this could be agreed on. Compromise was finally reached in a decision simply to increase reserves by means of special drawing rights on the IMF, to be granted if and when 85 per cent of voting power in the Fund decides that a shortage of reserves exists. These special rights, unlike the ordinary IMF quotas, would be counted as part of each country's official reserves; part of them would consist of permanent assets which would not be repaid, and they would nearly double the rate at which IMF drawings can add to world liquidity. This decision, although falling short of Anglo-American objectives, is still viewed as potentially highly inflationary by the French, who continue to believe that international liquidity should only consist of and be increased through gold, and appear to see nothing inconsistent in arguing that the price of gold should be doubled while maintaining that world liquidity cannot be increased through a new use or sort of reserve currencies, since 'there is no magic remedy. No one can produce international currency without someone paying for it.'[1]

The 1967 agreement was a tentative first step towards solving world liquidity problems. A further prospect of improvement in this respect was opened up at the same time by the renewal of the British application to join the EEC, since it had now become clear that the Six saw Britain's role as a reserve currency country as incompatible with membership. The obvious answer to this, which became increasingly discussed as a means of solving Britain's problems and at the same time satisfying the European desire for economic and political prestige more equal to that of the USA, is to substitute a joint European reserve currency. This could be achieved by the pooling of a proportion of all members' gold and dollar reserves with a European central bank, which would issue a new unit of account in exchange (usually called for purposes of illustration a Europa). Overseas holdings of sterling would gradually be replaced by Europas, Britain acquiring instead a debt to the central bank, which would have the advantage of being on fixed repayment terms instead of being subject to unpredictable demands for repayment. A reserve currency based on Europa's combined reserves would avoid the problems of one maintained by a single country, and a regional proposal of this nature might have a much better chance of agreement than one to solve the problems of sterling (or the dollar) by similar means but through world co-operation through the IMF. It depends, however, on Britain becoming a member of the EEC or at least forming some much closer ties with the member countries.

[1] M. Debré, the French Finance Minister, at the joint meeting of the World Bank and the IMF, September 1967.

If prospects for increasing world liquidity seemed to be improving, however, nothing had been achieved towards an international mechanism of adjustment in balance of payments problems, or towards international decisions on when changes in exchange rates are essential or towards international rescue operations through grants or long-term loans from surplus to deficit countries. Meanwhile, at the end of 1967, the British balance of payments deficit finally forced a devaluation of the £. This turned the attention of speculators to the possibility of devaluation of the other reserve currency, the dollar, for it was apparent that the US' falling gold reserves could not continue to supply the means for the government to continue to buy dollars for gold at the rate of $35 per ounce for very much longer. This realization led to an enormous rush to buy gold in the hope of an American devaluation, which would mean in effect an increase in the price of gold.

The gold crisis of the spring of 1968 made the prospect of the collapse of the international monetary system a real one, but it has not so far resulted in any agreement on a radical reform. The draining away of gold from official reserves into the hands of speculators was halted by the announcement of the 'two-tier' gold system; the central banks of the seven leading industrialized countries (France did not join in) announced that they would no longer sell gold to private buyers, while the US Treasury will continue to supply gold to these and other central banks at $35 an ounce as long as it is not resold at a profit to the private market. There is, therefore, now a free market price for gold not owned by central banks, and as long as this price does not rise so much above $35 as to tempt governments to break the agreement the crisis should not recur. In the long run, the survival of the present system depends on the USA managing to exert some control over its balance of payments problem; unless this happens speculation is bound to revive. The situation will be eased by the probable implementation next year of the special drawing rights in the IMF, but this again has been made conditional on an improvement in the balance of payments of the USA and the UK.

Economists in many countries would agree that the ultimate solution to international monetary problems probably lies in the creation of an international credit currency, controlled by a world central bank and independent of the vagaries of gold production or currency speculation, but the sacrifice of sovereignty involved is still too great for such a plan to be accepted. While governments have become much more accustomed in recent years to criticisms of their domestic economic policies by international institutions and by the monetary authorities of other countries, on whom they now depend for assistance at times of monetary difficulties, such dependence is nevertheless still resisted. Economic and political objectives among Western developed countries have moved much closer together, but differences are still evidently too great for international control to operate without many problems of policy arising between developed countries and towards the under-developed world.

CHAPTER FIFTEEN

The Problems of the Rich

THE PERSISTENCE OF POVERTY

'It now looks as though the rate of growth between 1964 and 1970 will be barely 15 per cent compared with the 25 per cent achieved in the previous six years under Conservative government. In addition to the cuts this must mean in the social programmes, the consumer will be affected still more severely. The difference between a total rate of growth of 15 per cent and 25 per cent in the six years up to 1970 is the difference between every family in the land being able to buy a new mini car, a fully automatic washing machine and a washing-up machine or their equivalent during that time, or going without them.'

(Edward Heath, leader of the British Opposition, quoted in *The Economist*, July 15, 1967.)

Most modern Western definitions of the subject of economics describe it as the study of the relationship between scarce resources and competing human wants. From the point of view of the underdeveloped world, it is hard to see that the rich countries of the West have any problems that can in this sense properly be described as economic. The problems of scarcity and of choice between the satisfaction of different needs which face the poor countries of Asia, Africa and South America are on a totally different level to those which occur in the countries of North America and Western Europe, and in the others normally considered to be 'developed', where economists have indeed begun to concern themselves at times with problems which relate not to scarcity but to abundance—such problems as arise when production has expanded beyond the satisfaction of obvious consumer wants, and consumers' desires appear to need to be created for the sake of maintaining production, or when technological advance brings about a situation in which human labour is no longer required for the greater part of a manufacturing process.

It is nevertheless the case, with very few exceptions, that the rich countries are still faced with severe problems of poverty at home, and in a sense with a scarcity of resources with which to deal with them. In the richest country of all, the USA, a government study carried out in 1960 defined one fifth of the population as poor. Poverty is of course a relative concept, and the income limit used as a definition—$4,000 per family or $2,000 per single person—would have implied prosperity elsewhere. But among these some 12·5 million people, or 7 per cent of the population, were found to have less than half of the 'poverty income', and with the additional fact of the high American cost of living these figures point to the existence of poverty by any standards, the poverty of malnutrition, inadequate clothing, insanitary housing and the accompanying ill health.

Such pockets of poverty are to be found in nearly all developed countries, since high average incomes per head do not necessarily mean that national income is in any way evenly distributed. Earnings still vary widely between occupations, even though not as widely as in the underdeveloped world. The greatest poverty tends however to be concentrated among households distinguished by other factors than occupation—outstandingly by the unemployment, sickness or old age of the head of the household, by its consisting of a woman bringing up children on her own, or by the existence of a large number of children in combination with any of these problems or where the father is in a low-wage occupation. The extent and severity of poverty in any one developed country consequently depends mainly on two aspects of its economic organization; the degree of unemployment which is tolerated by its government, and the proportion of its national income which is devoted to social security arrangements (together with the efficiency of such arrangements). As we saw in Chapter 9, most of the rich countries of Europe have had unemployment levels of under $2\frac{1}{2}$ per cent of the total labour force ever since 1950. In these countries, poverty caused by unemployment is nationally on a very small scale, although regionally, as for example in Northern Ireland in relation to the UK, it is sometimes severe. In the USA, on the other hand, a national unemployment rate ranging from 4 to 7 per cent has been normal, and there is still appreciable poverty based on unemployment. The developed countries also differ greatly in their provisions for social security. As a proportion of gross national product, spending on social services in the leading industrialized countries ranged in 1965 from just over 11 per cent in the UK (which suffers from a delusion that it is a very high spender in this respect) to nearly 14 per cent in West Germany; the American proportion was about 12 per cent. However, in both Britain and the USA the proportion of gross national product used to pay out cash benefits to those in need is very much smaller than in most European countries. In Britain, a very large proportion of welfare spending is devoted to the provision of a free national health service, covering the entire population. No other European country provides such a service, although some sort of official medical insurance providing the greater part of fees normally covers at least 80 per cent of the population; in the USA free medical treatment is provided for those over 65 and for others qualifying as needy. Poverty is, however, much more generally affected by the cash benefits paid to the old, the unemployed and the sick, and in the form of family allowances, and in this respect far more generous provision is made in most European countries than in the UK or the USA, or as a rule in Australia and New Zealand. The social security system operated in most of Europe is based on the insurance principle, financed almost wholly by employers and employees by contributions paid in relation to earnings and providing benefits also in relation to earnings. The basic aim of British social security, on the other hand, is to provide flat rate benefits at a subsistence minimum, and these are still mainly financed by flat rate contributions paid by employers (who pay much less than in Europe) and by employees, with supplements from general taxation. In several European countries, old age pensions constitute a much higher percentage of past earnings than in the UK, and they are moreover automatically adjusted for changes in the cost of living or in the wage index. Sickness and unemployment benefits similarly are usually higher in most countries in relation to normal earnings, and family allowances are also paid at a much higher level. No family allowances are paid in the USA, and only four states operate sickness benefit schemes. Unemployment benefits tend to be rather lower than in the UK. In Britain, a much higher proportion of welfare spending than anywhere else is directed to 'national assistance', the system intended as a safety net by means of which the incomes of those inadequately provided for by the other social security schemes can be brought up to subsistence level. Research into the causes of poverty has however always tended to show that this system at least as it stands is hard to operate in such a way as to eliminate real distress.

While all the developed countries continue to face some problems of poverty among their own inhabitants, some have been much more successful in reducing them than others. Nevertheless no rich country can be described as content with its achievement in this respect, and it is indeed those countries which spend the greatest proportions of their incomes on the most elaborate social security schemes which tend to be most concerned with the need for further improvements, just as it is those countries which have had the least unemployment over the last two decades which are most worried about any increase in unemployment rates. But with spending on social security already amounting to well over 10 per cent of national income in most of these countries, any substantial improvement must mean a substantial cut elsewhere— in the expenditure of richer consumers, in public current spending or in investment, unless it can be derived from an increase in national income itself.

In recent years, the leading industrialized countries have also become increasingly aware of their own poverty in another area of economic life. This is the area of public provision of services which consumers (and companies) do not expect to provide for themselves. Its boundaries vary from country to country, but they normally include the greater part of education and a substantial proportion of health services, all arrangements for maintaining law and order, some aspects of transport and communications, and the provision of some of the cheapest housing. In some countries a significant part of entertainment and recreation is involved, together with public patronage of the arts, and an increasingly important aspect in most countries in recent years has been the public financing of scientific and technological research. Just as with poverty among individuals, the concept of the developed countries' poverty in public services is relative; they are of course extremely wealthy in this respect in relation to any underdeveloped country, and as far as most public services are concerned in relation to the communist countries as well. The example in some instances of the USSR and the richer Eastern European countries has nevertheless reminded the west of the higher priority which can be given to the development of public services by a wealthy authoritarian régime, while individual western countries have set examples to each other in other cases. The main reason for the growing discontent with this aspect of western economic life is, however, not so much international rivalries as the ever-increasing contrast at home between public and private standards.

The greatest contrasts between 'private affluence and public squalor' have arisen in the country with the highest standard of private living, the USA, and their best known exponent, Professor J. K. Galbraith, describes the American situation in particular. 'Economists in calculating the total output of the economy—in arriving at the now familiar Gross National Product —add together the value of all goods and services of whatever sort and by whomsoever produced. No distinction is made between public and privately produced services. An increased supply of educational services has a standing in the total not different in kind from an increased output of television receivers. . . . In the general view it is privately produced production that is important, and that nearly alone. . . . Such attitudes lead to interesting contradictions. Cars have an importance greater than the roads on which they are driven. We welcome expansion of telephone services[1] as improving the general well-being, but accept curtailment of postal services as signifying necessary economy. We set great store by the increase in private wealth but regret the added outlays for the police force by which it is protected. Vacuum cleaners to ensure clean houses are praiseworthy and essential in our standard of living. Street cleaners to

---

[1] Telephone services in the USA are provided by private enterprise.

ensure clean streets are an unfortunate expense. Partly as a result, our houses are generally clean and our streets generally filthy.'[1] In fact there is undoubtedly concern with the need to improve public services even in a country as ideologically committed to private enterprise as the USA, while other developed countries, notably in Scandinavia, have had a very different scale of priorities for some time. As the average inhabitant of a developed country becomes more accustomed to the immediate satisfaction of his private needs, he becomes less and less willing to tolerate public squalor, and the most urgent pressure for improvement is felt currently in the countries of Western Europe such as the UK, France and West Germany, where consumer prosperity is relatively recent and many public services relatively poor.

These countries often seem at the present time to be confronted with a direct choice between a further increase in private or in public standards. In Britain for example it was decided recently (to take one of Galbraith's contrasting examples) to introduce colour television services, and manufacturers of television sets forecast a rise in annual sales of colour sets to half a million by 1973. At a price approaching £300 a set, this will represent an expenditure in that year of nearly £150 million. The average annual cost of the school building programme for the five years 1961–66 was originally estimated at £73 million, under half this amount, which left well over a million children in schools built before the 1914–18 war. Such contrasts—when observed—lead many consumers to question the economic priorities of their society.

However, in all the countries of Western Europe public expenditure for social purposes has in fact been growing appreciably faster in recent years than national income. Public current spending and public investment already usually account for at least a quarter of national output, so that once again any substantial increase must mean a substantial cut in private expenditure, or else be derived from an increase in national income itself. The only other possibility is a redistribution within government

[1] J. K. Galbraith, *The Affluent Society*, Hamish Hamilton, 1958.

spending itself. It is frequently pointed out that world disarmament would release nearly 10 per cent of GNP, in the case of the USA, and some 7 per cent in the case of most of the richer countries of Western Europe, to add to social expenditure and investment at home and to aid to underdeveloped countries abroad.

THE NEED TO MAINTAIN GROWTH

The economic ambitions of the developed countries have partly for these reasons advanced from the post-war goals of avoiding periodic depressions and heavy unemployment to achieving and sustaining a large annual increase in national income. Such increases are needed to eliminate the remaining poverty among their inhabitants, to improve public services to the level required by populations accustomed to high private standards and increasingly able to make their wants known, and also if any further addition is to be made to the help given to underdeveloped countries. These objects apart, it is now felt that a country which is unable to show a substantial annual increase in output is slipping back towards the problems of the 1930's. Merely to sustain the level of production is not enough; in modern conditions growth is essential in order to ensure that a high proportion of national income is reinvested in new capacity and in new knowledge and skills, without which a developed economy will rapidly cease to be competitive with others.

Chapter 9 outlined the arguments of economists who believe that there is no reason why developed economies should not now maintain a high rate of growth more or less indefinitely. These arguments have been under close examination in 1967, which showed a marked slowing down of growth in Europe, notably in West Germany and in the UK. It has been shown that in these circumstances governments can still be reluctant to make use of Keynesian methods to stimulate production; the West German authorities because of their fear of inflation, and the British government because it feels bound to give its balance of payments problems priority over those of growth. On the other hand the

US government has made a successful use of tax cuts over recent years to stimulate demand and hence production, and has achieved the lowest rate of unemployment for several years. In the short run, countries without severe balance of payments difficulties can solve their growth problems by Keynesian remedies, while balance of payments problems must as we saw in Chapter 14 depend largely on international solutions. In the longer run, however, Keynesian remedies are not wholly adequate to deal with the modern problem of inflation, which accompanies full employment; it is no longer politically acceptable for governments to effect a cure by reducing demand to the point at which unemployment becomes high enough. Developed countries today with rapidly growing economies are constantly faced with the difficulty of how to prevent wages and prices rising so fast as to cancel out much of the increase in production, or to prevent wages from rising regardless of the behaviour of productivity. Internally, a modest inflation is not necessarily more than an inconvenience, since in the kind of inflation which takes place under full employment wages keep up with prices, and provided some means can be found of protecting those inhabitants, such as pensioners, with fixed incomes, no hardships need be suffered. But governments are bound to be concerned if their export prices rise faster than those of their competitors, while imports become increasingly cheaper in relation to domestic products. Hence the especial preoccupation of governments with balance of payments problems with the need to limit inflation. In recent years several attempts have been made to do this by means of policies to limit the total increase in incomes to something less than the total growth in productivity. This kind of economic control is of course preferable to a cure by cutting back demand and increasing unemployment, and it is internationally preferable to placing restrictions on imports. So far, however, no government has managed to impose an incomes policy for long.

There is another criticism of the ability of Keynesian economics to provide a long-term solution to the problems of economic growth, which perhaps occurs more often to non-economists than economists. This is expressed in a tendency to mistrust a system which seems ultimately to rest on production for its own sake rather than for consumers' needs. Keynes explained that the way to avoid unemployment was to stimulate demand and so give rise to higher production; once this method of economic control is applied to the goal of maintaining a high rate of growth rather than simply to eliminate serious depressions, the implication is that demand must be stimulated to higher and higher levels, ever further from what the current generation has been accustomed to think of as necessary or even desirable. In fact as we have seen most developed countries still have very considerable scope for increasing output to satisfy obvious needs. Nevertheless there are sectors of industry in these countries which already seem to depend on the creation of artificial wants by means of intensive advertising or—one of the most startling aspects of the affluent society —the built-in obsolescence of their products. It is understandable to question the permanence of an economic system which seems about to become based on the willingness of consumers to repurchase every few years goods which could be made to last for a lifetime. However, it may be observed that it is only in this century that most of the inhabitants of developed countries have grown used to the idea of more or less annual purchases of new clothes and the throwing away of old ones. Just as it now seems unusual to wear the same clothes for the whole of adult life, and bizarre to inherit them from parents, there is no reason why it should not seem normal to discard furniture, refrigerators and motor cars at an equally rapid rate; the real objection to this is that at present, in relation to the needs of the poor at home and abroad, and to some of the unsatisfied needs of the relatively rich, it is an appalling waste of resources.

The other question mark over the future of the affluent societies of the west is raised by the advance of automation. When increased production can be achieved without any increase in labour, the Keynesian solution to depression ceases to apply. Until recently, technological advance has always meant higher general prosperity[1]—higher demand, higher output, higher wages and shorter working hours. The countries of Western Europe, at least, have

[1] Except of course at the very beginning of the industrial revolution, when the introduction of machinery for spinning and weaving did initially cause unemployment.

continued to be short of all kinds of labour, even the unskilled. But in the USA some part of the percentage of unemployment is now described as 'structural', i.e. it consists of workers with no skills living in regions in which there is no prospect of any further increase in demand for unskilled labour, or of workers with skills once useful but now no longer in demand. Some of this redundancy is derived from the progress of automation, which the government has estimated as eliminating some 50,000 jobs a year. Its effects have been most evident in the mining industries, and in steel and textile mills, but it has also now begun to affect employment in a wide variety of other manufacturing industries, in building and in clerical work. The US government became sufficiently concerned with this trend in 1964 to set up a National Commission on Technology, Automation and Economic Progress. The Commission has pointed out that the problems raised by automation can certainly theoretically be solved by government action to share out the gains from increased productivity, such as through state subsidies to ensure a minimum income for every household and state finance to provide extra employment through the expansion of public services, particularly in hospitals and schools. Above all, a large extension of free higher education, and of all forms of technical training and retraining to match the labour force to the new requirements, would enable the new technology to be expanded and applied to give rise to all sorts of new occupations in connection with what the Commission described as 'unfinished social tasks', particularly in public health. The change in political attitudes implied in such a programme would of course be very considerable for the USA, with its tradition of reducing the economic role of government to a minimum. It would be relatively simple for the more left-wing countries of Western Europe, but these are further from having to face the problem, although some of them are gaining experience of dealing with structural unemployment caused by declining industries and in depressed regions, and are becoming accustomed to government action to regulate redundancy and in the field of retraining and encouragement of labour to move between occupations and areas. It would be easiest of all for the communist countries, who are certainly the best placed to solve the problems of affluence when they arrive; they see no obstacles to the re-allocation either of work or of its proceeds.

INTERNATIONAL CO-OPERATION

As the preceding chapters have shown, the economic prospects for rich and poor countries alike now depend very much on international co-operation in various economic as well as political spheres. Most underdeveloped countries have little hope of achieving higher standards of living without the continued injection of capital and technical assistance from the developed, and from the point of view of both recipient and donor countries aid can be much more effectively supplied and used when it is not merely on a nation-to-nation basis. The enormous increase in the prosperity of the developed countries over the last two decades has derived to a large extent from a new level of international organization to reduce barriers to trade; the greatest potential setback to their future growth would be a reversal of this trend, and in particular a failure to solve international monetary problems before world liquidity requirements outrun world reserves. The two developed countries which currently have the most outstanding economic problems, the UK and the USA, are the countries burdened with what should be an internationally managed responsibility, the provision of an international reserve currency.

The years since 1945 have been a time of unprecedented international co-operation, and it is not surprising that with so much more attempted there should have been frequent setbacks. It is possible to argue from these that the prospects for the future are poor; that international co-operation to increase the flow of trade is being replaced by regional blocs, that agreement on international monetary reform is unlikely to be reached, and that governments' new-found techniques of controlling their own economies are bound to lead to an economic nationalism working against the previous trend. At the same time, it is hard to believe that the enormous gains of the last two decades could be allowed to be eroded, particularly while the third of the world which lies under a different political and economic system continues to challenge the Western democracies to show better results. Just as in the course of their industrialization the developed countries gradually learnt that the uncontrolled pursuit of their own interests by individuals was no guarantee of the economic welfare of the nation as a whole, with the achievement of prosperity they are in the process of learning that national interests are better served within a system of international economic controls.

Bibliography and Further Reading

GENERAL

P. T. ELLSWORTH: *The International Economy*, Macmillan, New York 1953.

A. J. BROWN: *Introduction to the World Economy*, Unwin University Books 1965.

W. W. ROSTOW: *The Stages of Economic Growth*, CUP 1960.

ON DEVELOPED COUNTRIES, THEIR ECONOMIC
HISTORY AND PRESENT DAY PROBLEMS

T. K. DERRY, *A Short Economic History of Britain*, OUP 1965.

P. J. D. WILES: *The Political Economy of Communism*, Harvard UP 1962.

H. SCHWARTZ: *The Soviet Economy since Stalin*, J. B. Lippincott, Philadelphia and New York 1964.

G. MYRDAL: *Beyond the Welfare State*, Duckworth and Co Ltd 1960, and *Challenge to Affluence*, Gollancz 1964.

J. K. GALBRAITH: *The Affluent Society*, Hamish Hamilton 1958.

A. SCHONFIELD: *Modern Capitalism*, R.I.I.A., OUP 1965.

ON UNDERDEVELOPED COUNTRIES AND
COLONIALISM

H. MYINT: *The Economics of the Developing Countries*, Hutchinson University Library 1965.

T. BALOGH: *The Economics of Poverty*, Weidenfeld and Nicolson 1966.

A. SCHONFIELD: *The Attack on World Poverty*, Chatto and Windus 1961.

G. Myrdal: *Economic Theory and Underdeveloped Regions*, Duckworth 1957.

R. Dumont: *False Start in Africa*, André Deutsch 1966.

S. C. Easton: *The Rise and Fall of Western Colonialism*, Pall Mall Press 1964.

R. Oliver & J. D. Fage: *A Short History of Africa*, Penguin African Library 1962.

P. Mason: *The Birth of a Dilemma*, OUP 1958.

M. Perham: *Lugard*, Volumes I and II, Collins 1956.

ON CURRENT INTERNATIONAL PROBLEMS:
MONETARY REFORM, TRADE AND AID

H. G. Johnson: *The World Economy at the Cross Roads*, Clarendon Press 1965.

S. Dell: *Trade Blocs and Common Markets*, Constable 1963.

H. G. Grubel: *World Monetary Reform*, Stanford University Press, California 1963.

F. Machlup: *Plans for the Reform of the International Monetary System*, Princeton University, Department of Economics 1964.

J. D. Rowe: *Primary Commodities in International Trade*, Cambridge 1965.

I. M. D. Little & J. M. Clifford: *International Aid*, Allen and Unwin 1965.

Index

'Adjustment' problem, 182
Africa, arbitrary frontiers in, 97
  project-tying in, 140
Agricultural surpluses, gifts of, 126 f.
Agriculture, in China, 73
  Colonial, introduced crops, 97
  in EEC, 150
  in Russia, 66, 67, 69, 114
  in Yugoslavia, 71
Aid, passing on cost of, 139
  procurement tying, 140–1
  project tying, 140
  technical assistance, 141
  value of, 138
Alliance for Progress, 167
Armaments, 26
Artificial wants, 199
Asbestos, sources, 22
Automation, effect of, 199

'Basle Group', 181
Benelux, customs union, 107
Birth rates, 123–4
Boundaries, of states, without economic meaning, 13
Brazil, coffee agreement, 167
Bretton Woods, 102, 103
Britain, aid given by 132–4, 136
  between the wars, 76
  separation from Europe, 107
Budgets, balancing of, 81
Buffer stock, 162
Burdensome surpluses, 161
Bureaucracy, in Russia, 72

Capital, movements of, 37
Capitalist economies, Government control in, 113
China, 17
  communism in, 72
  Great Leap Forward, 74
  population per square mile, 21
Coal reserves, 22
Cobalt, sources, 22
Cocoa, agreement on, 168
Coconuts, production of, 24
Colour television, 196
Colonial Development Fund, 94
Colonialism, balance sheets of, 95

twentieth-century, 91
  distortion of economy by, 99
  economics of, 86
  non-economic purposes, 89
  Russian, 95 f.
Colonies, early barter in, 96
  forms of government, 97–8
  withdrawal from, 98
Committee of European Co-operation, 106
Commodity agreements, 161
  value of, 168
Common Market, proposed, in Africa, 158
Commonwealth Sugar Agreement, 163
Communism (See also Marxism),
  in China, 72
  competition with the West, 113
  in Russia, 64
  and underdeveloped countries, 122–123
  after World War II, 70
Communist countries, aid given by, 137
  consumer goods in, 26
  exports, 35, 36
  income per head, 17
  public services in, 195
Communist planning, 64
  aim of, 14
Comparative advantage, theory of, 31
Comparative cost, in international trade, 39
Complementary countries, 32
Congo, forced labour in, 97
  independence of, 130
Consumer goods, from interchangeable parts, 47
Consumers' wants, in Communist economies, 15
Consumption, 25
  in developed and underdeveloped economies, 27
Copper, sources, 22
Copper industry, capital and labour in, 24
Cultivation, area of 21–2
Currency revaluations, 183
Customs unions, 104 f.

Death rates, 124
Depression, Great, of 1930's, 76
    causes, 78
Devaluation, of £, 189
Developed countries, 15, 17
    exports, 35
    post-war prosperity, 109
    poverty in, 192
Developing countries, 17
Development Assistance Group, 116
Dillon round, 152
Diseases, tropical, research on, 96
Drive to maturity, 17
Dumping, new definition, 153
Durable consumer goods, 25

East African Common Market, 159, 160
East Germany, 17
Economic infrastructure, 17
Economic progress, 18
Economic resources, 20
Economies, centrally planned, (communist), 14
    consumption patterns, 26
    developed, 14
    five stages of development, 17
    groups of, 13
    post-war II, 101
    primary, 14
    underdeveloped, 14
'Economism' in China, 75
Economy, definition, 13
    as political organization, 13
Education, in colonial territories, 92–3
Empire Free Trade, 93
Employment, control of level of, 82
Europas (unit of currency), 188
Europe, unification of, 105
l'Europe des Patries, concept, 148
European Coal and Steel Community, 107
European Common Market, and free trade, 32
    overseas preferences, 127
European Economic Community, 145, 146
    diverse interests in, 147–8
    trade in, 149
European Free Trade Area, 108, 112, 145
    and free trade, 32
    success of, 152
European Payments Union, 106
Exploitation, Marxian theory of, 63

Factories, growth of, 46
Factory Acts, 55

Family allowances, 193–4
Farm support programmes, 147
Fibres, hard, export restrictions, 167
Five Year Plans, 68
Food prices, in EEC 150–1
France, aid given by, 132, 133, 134, 136
Free enterprise, in Britain and the U.S., 53
Free Trade, theories, 32
Free trade areas, 104 f.

GATT. General Agreement on Tariffs and Trade, 104, 112, 127, 145, 160, 161
Gold, two-tier system, 189
Gold crisis, 187
Gold Standard, 58, 77, 79, 174–5, 182, 185
Governments, economic intervention during First World War, 59
    functions of, traditional, 52
    intervention in economics, 54
    level of investment by, 111
    ownership by, 14
Greece, 17
    low income per head, 15

Havana Charter, 104, 161, 162, 165, 166, 168
Hire purchase, Government regulation, 81
Household expenditure, 27, 28
Housing, slum, 48

Imperial preference, 93
India, 15
    administration taken over from East India Co., 88
    aid for, 136
    exports, 35
    population per square mile, 21
Industrialization, attitude to, 46
    progress of, 45
Infant industry argument, 31
Inflation and full employment, 198
International aid, 39
International Clearing Union, plan, 176
International Coffee Agreement, 165, 171
International complementarity, decline in, 33
International co-operation, 201
International Development Association, 116, 138
International Finance Corporation, 138

International Monetary Fund, 80, 102
  operation of, 174, 177
  reserves held, 179
International Monetary System, proposals for reform, 183
International Sugar Agreement, 163
International Tin Agreement, 164
International trade, patterns of, 32
  theory, 29
International Trade Organization, 104
International Wheat Agreement, 162
Investment, productivity of, 15
Investments abroad, 37
Inward-looking industrialization, 158
Iron ore resources, 22
Italy, as developed country, 15

Japan, as developed country, 15
  production in, 23

Kennedy round, 152
Keynes, J. M. (Lord), 57, 79, 103, 162, 176, 178, 198, 199
Khruschev, agriculture under, 71–2
Kidric, Boris, 71

Labour, international movement of, 111
  and natural resources, 23
  redeployment, 40
  skilled, 24
Laissez Faire, theory, 52
  alternatives to, 79
  erosion of, 54
Latin America Free Trade Area, 32, 158
League of Nations, on colonies, 92
Lend-Lease, 102 f.

Manual dexterity, 20
Marshall aid, 105, 106, 135
Marxism, (See also Communism), 61
  view of colonialism, 86
Mass-consumption, age of, 17
Mineral resources, 22
Monetary policies, national, 175, 176
Monopolies, of underdeveloped countries, 173
Multiplier concept, 81

NEP. See New Economic Policy
National Commission on Technology, Automation and Economic Progress, 200
National income, 15
  gross, 16
  in underdeveloped economies, 16

National insurance, 56
National Recovery Act (U.S.) 83
National wealth, or poverty, 20
Natural resources, distribution of, 21
Neo-colonialism, 37
  of U.S. 95 f.
New Economic Policy (USSR), 67
Nickel, sources, 22

Obsolescence, built-in, 199
Old Age pensions, 56, 193
Opportunity cost, 40
Organization for Economic Co-operation and Development 106 f.
Organization for European Economic Co-operation, 106, 112

Pattern of production, freezing of, 172
Petroleum, reserves, 22
Pig iron, growth of, 47
Poland, relaxation of Stalinism in, 71
Population, of communist, developed and underdeveloped countries, 21
  growth of, 123
  in America, 47
  per square mile, 21
Portugal, 17
  low income per head, 15
Poverty, at home and abroad, 18
  persistence of, 191
Production, 23
  decisions, 24
  for investment, 26
Productivity, rise in Europe, 112
'Propensity to consume', 80
Public services, 194
Purchase tax, value-added, 147 f.

Reparations, 59
Research, financing of, 195
Reserve currencies, 175
  joint European, 188
Returns to scale, 25
Rhodesia, annexation of, 91 f.
Rome Treaty, 108, 146, 147
Russia, 17
  aid to underdeveloped countries, 117
  development between the wars, 84
  economic policy after Stalin, 114
  income per head, 16
  self-sufficiency, 29

Scandinavia, priorities in, 196
Schuman Plan, 107
Services, public and private
  production in, 195

Social security in developed countries, 193
Social security system, in EEC, 147
Socialism, 55
effect of World War I, 60
South Africa, 17
South America, population, 21
Special U.N. Fund for Economic Development, proposed, 109
Stalinism, 68
agriculture under, 69
in China, 73
heavy industries under, 69
repudiated, 71
Standards of living, 48
Steel, countries producing, 25
Suez crisis, 164, 165, 181
Sugar, West Indies, 97
Surplus production, accumulation of, 172
Surplus value, 63
Synthetics, proposed restriction of research, 171
substitutes, 36

Take-off, and pre-conditions for, 17
Tariffs, 31
against underdeveloped countries, 156–7
cuts in, effects, 35
in EEC, 146, 149
expansion of, 82, 83
on tropical agricultural products, 156
Tea, skill in production of, 24
Tin, sources, 22
Trade unions, membership, 56
Trading blocs, 145
European, 146
underdeveloped countries, 158
Transport, mechanization of, 46

Underdeveloped countries, after World War II, 102
aid for, 115
criteria for, 137
purpose of, 131
cartels suggested for, 171
exports, 35
and international trade, 126

monopolies of, 173
population problems, 124–5
trade of, 36, 145
trading between, 157
Western attitude to, 121
and World trade, 154
Undernutrition, 123
Unemployment, exportability, 79
in Britain, 77
'structural', 200
in United States, 78
World, 79
Unemployment Act, 77
Unemployment benefit, 194
United Nations Charter, 102
United Nations Conference on Trade and Development, 128, 143, 155
United Nations Special Fund, 115
United Nations Trust Territories, 95
United States, aid given by, 133–4, 136
between the wars, 77
investment abroad, 38
poverty in, 192
self-sufficiency of, 29
United States Trade Expansion Act, 153
Uranium, sources, 22

Value-added turnover tax, 147
Venezuela, state of development, 15

Wages, in 1913, 50
rise in, 49
War communism (in Russia), 66
War socialism (in Britain), 60
West Germany, aid given by, 131, 132, 133, 136
World Bank, 102, 103, 138, 140
World Economic Conference, 84
World exports, 34
World Health Organization, 125
World trade, liberalization, 145
World War I, 56
cost of, 58
economic consequences, 57

Yugoslavia, 17
communism in, 70